The Ultimate Diabetic
Cookbook After 50

A Complete Diabetic Diet Guide with Delicious and Low Sugar Recipes, Incl. 6-Week Meal Plan and Shopping List for Diabetes After 50 to Live Better

Sophy Warlante

Copyright © 2024 By Sophy Warlante
All rights reserved.

No part of this book may be reproduced, transmitted,
or distributed in any form or by any means
without permission in writing from
the publisher except in the case of brief quotations embodied
in critical articles or reviews.

Legal & Disclaimer

The content and information in this book is
consistent and truthful,
and it has been provided for informational,
educational and business purposes only.

The illustrations in the book are from the
website shutterstock.com,
depositphoto.com and freepik.
com and have been authorized.

The content and information contained
in this book has been compiled from reliable sources,
which are accurate based on the knowledge,
belief, expertise and information of the Author.
The author cannot be held liable for
any omissions and/or errors.

TABLE OF CONTENT

INTRODUCTION 1

Chapter 1: Managing Diabetes After 50 3

Differences in Diabetes: Older Adults vs. Younger Individuals 3
Basics of Diabetes After 50 4
Nutritional Needs for Those Over 50 5
Tips and Strategies for Managing Diabetes ... 7
Meal Plan and Shopping List 8
Tips for Dining Out 9

Chapter 2: Breakfast 10

Pumpkin Pancakes 10
Chia Pudding with Fruits 10
Poached Eggs & Grits 11
Healthy Buckwheat Crêpes 11
Ratatouille Egg Bake 12
Cheese Mushroom Frittata 12
Walnut and Oat Granola 13
Peanut Butter Waffles 13
Coconut and Blueberry Oatmeal 14
Spinach & Tomato Egg Muffins 14

Chapter 3: Fish and Seafood 15

Parchment-Paper Halibut with Lemon 15
Cod with Asparagus 15
Mahi Mahi with Green Beans 16
Spicy Shrimp Kebabs 16
Easy Mediterranean Scallops 17
Haddock Tacos with Cabbage 17
Baked Flounder with Brussels Sprouts 18
Cod Chowder with Cauliflower 18
Shrimp Ceviche with Avocado 19
Monkfish in Tomato Sauce 19

Chapter 4: Vegetables 20

Zoodles with Mediterranean Sauce 20
Spiced Eggplant 20
Roasted Asparagus with Almonds 21
Stir Fried Zucchini and Bell Pepper 21
Creamy Spinach with Mushrooms 22
Sweet and Spicy Cauliflower 22
Zucchini Fritters 23
Spaghetti Squash Noodles with Tomatoes.... 23
Broccoli Rabe with Cilantro and Red Pepper 24
Spinach with Olives 24

Chapter 5: Bean and Legumes 25

Tomato and White Beans with Spinach 25
Rosemary White Beans 25
Triple Bean Chili 26
Red Kidney Beans with Green Beans 26
Herbs Kidney Bean Stew 27
Black-Eyed Peas and Carrot Curry 27
Pearl Barley and Black Beans Stew 28
Roasted Eggplant and Cannellini Beans 28
Green Lentil and Carrot Stew 29
Herbed Black Beans 29

Chapter 6: Egg Dishes 30

Asparagus Frittata with Goat Cheese 30
Classic Shakshuka 30
Hard-Boiled Eggs with Cayenne Pepper 31
Veggie-Packed Scrambled Eggs 31
Spinach and Feta Omelet 32
Crust Less Broccoli Quiche 32
Poached Eggs with Sautéed Kale and Mushrooms 33
Avocado and Egg Breakfast Bowl 33
Low-Carb Egg Muffins 34
Egg and Cucumber Salad Wrap 34

Chapter 7: Poultry 35

Cheese and Spinach Stuffed Chicken Breasts 35
Fried Eggplant with Chicken 35
Thyme Chicken Breasts and Brussels Sprouts 36
Spicy Chicken and Tomatoes 36

Chicken and Veggie Kabobs 37
Jamaican Curry Chicken Drumsticks 37
Spiced Roasted Whole Chicken................. 38
Creamy Chicken with Mushrooms 38
Buffalo Chicken Wings 39
Crispy Herbed Turkey Breast..................... 39

Chapter 8: Lean Meats and Tofu 40
Garlicky Tofu and Brussels Sprouts 40
Beef and Cauliflower 40
Tofu and Broccoli Stir-Fry.......................... 41
Healthy Tempeh Lettuce Wraps................ 41
Curried Tofu 42
Pork Tenderloin with Paprika-Mustard 42
Teriyaki Tofu Burger 43
Beef Tips with Portobello Mushrooms 43
Grilled Tofu Skewers 44
Sun-dried Tomato Crusted Chops 44

Chapter 9: Salads 45
Rice Cauliflower Tabbouleh Salad............. 45
Quick Summer Chicken Salad 45
Lemony Kale and Tomato Salad 46
Endive and Shrimp with Walnuts.............. 46
Healthy Southwestern Salad..................... 47
Shredded Beef Salad................................. 47
Fresh Raspberry Spinach Salad 48
Thai Chicken Salad 48
Healthy Tuna Salad 49
Grilled Romaine Salad with Walnuts 49

Chapter 10: Soup and Stew... 50
Spicy Butternut Squash Soup.................... 50
Chicken and Zoodles Soup 50
Beef and Cabbage Stew 51
Carrot and Mushroom Soup 51
Thai Coconut Shrimp Soup 52
Chickpea, Zucchini and Kale Soup............. 52
Kale and Chicken Soup.............................. 53
Salmon and Spinach Stew......................... 53
Swiss Chard and Leek Soup....................... 54
Turkey Meatball and Kale Soup 54

Chapter 11: Drinks and Smoothies 55
Summer Cucumber Smoothie 55
Hemp Seed Milk 55
Avocado Smoothie.................................... 56
Energy Booster 56
Peanut Butter Papaya Chocolate Smoothie
.... 57
Vanilla Cold Butter Latte 57
Strawberry & Kiwi Smoothie 58
Ginger Detox Juice 58
Spicy Tomato Drink 59
Quick Peaches and Greens Smoothie 59

Chapter 12: Snacks 60
Roasted Chickpeas with Herbs.................. 60
Crispy Apple Chips 60
Buffalo Cauliflower Bites 61
Asian Chicken Wings................................. 61
Peach Bruschetta with Tarragon 62
Spicy Nuts 62
Healthy Almond Crackers......................... 63
Black Bean Stuffed Mini Peppers.............. 63
Roasted Cherry Tomato with Cheese........ 64
Garlicky Carrot with Toasted Almonds 64

Chapter 13: Appetizers and Sides 65
Classic Baba Ghanoush 65
Brussels Sprouts with Sesame 65
Smokey Garbanzo Mash 66
Cilantro Lime Cauliflower Rice 66
Steamed Artichoke with Aioli Sauce 67
Curried Cauliflower................................... 67
Sun Dried Tomato Hummus...................... 68
Pesto Spaghetti Squash 68
Green Broccolini Sauté 69
Spicy Mole Chicken Bites 69

Appendix 1: Basic Kitchen Conversions & Equivalents 70

Appendix 2: The Dirty Dozen and Clean Fifteen 71

Appendix 3: Recipes Index.. 72

INTRODUCTION

As I approached my 50s, I began to notice how my body responded differently to the foods I loved. It was a time of reflection and change, and after being diagnosed with diabetes, I realized I needed to adapt my diet to maintain my health while still enjoying my meals. This cookbook is a result of that journey—a collection of recipes and insights tailored for those of us navigating diabetes in our later years.

I remember feeling overwhelmed at first. There was so much information out there, and it seemed challenging to find meals that were not only healthy but also satisfying. I knew I wanted to focus on whole foods, balanced nutrients, and, most importantly, flavors that brought joy to my table. Cooking became my creative outlet, a way to explore new ingredients and techniques while taking control of my health.

Throughout this process, I discovered that eating well doesn't have to be boring or restrictive. In fact, it can be quite the opposite! I began experimenting with spices, fresh herbs, and seasonal produce, all of which enhanced the dishes I created. This cookbook is filled with recipes that highlight these vibrant ingredients, each designed to support healthy blood sugar levels without sacrificing taste.

I've also included practical tips and strategies that have worked for me along the way. From meal prepping to smart shopping, I want to share the lessons I've learned about making informed choices in the kitchen. You'll find advice on portion control, carbohydrate counting, and balancing your plate—tools that have empowered me to take charge of my health.

What I love most about cooking now is the sense of community it brings. Sharing meals with friends and family has become even more meaningful, and I've found that many people are eager to join me on this journey. With this cookbook, I hope to inspire you to invite loved ones to the table, fostering connections while enjoying delicious, diabetes-friendly meals.

So, whether you're newly diagnosed, have been managing diabetes for years, or simply want to eat healthier as you age, I invite you to dive into these pages. Let's explore the world of nutritious and flavorful cooking together, embracing this new chapter with enthusiasm and creativity. Here's to delicious meals that nourish both body and soul!

CHAPTER 1: MANAGING DIABETES AFTER 50

As we transition into our 50s and beyond, our bodies naturally undergo a variety of changes that can impact our overall health. For those diagnosed with diabetes, effective management becomes increasingly vital. The importance of managing diabetes at this stage cannot be overstated; it plays a critical role in minimizing the risk of complications and enhancing quality of life.

One significant concern for older adults with diabetes is the heightened risk of complications such as cardiovascular disease, neuropathy, and kidney problems. Research indicates that individuals over 50 are more susceptible to these complications due to factors like decreased organ function and a slower metabolic rate. By actively managing blood sugar levels through diet, exercise, and medication, you can significantly reduce the likelihood of these serious health issues. This proactive approach not only helps in maintaining physical health but also contributes to longevity.

Additionally, effective diabetes management fosters an overall improved quality of life. With the right strategies, you can maintain your energy levels, promote better sleep, and enhance your physical mobility. As you engage in activities you love—whether it's gardening, traveling, or spending time with family—managing your diabetes enables you to participate fully without the burdens of fatigue or health complications. This period of life is often filled with opportunities for personal growth and exploration, and proper management allows you to embrace these experiences without reservation.

The emotional and psychological dimensions of living with diabetes also warrant attention. Many older adults may experience feelings of isolation, anxiety, or frustration related to their condition. Managing diabetes effectively can alleviate these feelings by providing a sense of control over one's health. Educating yourself about diabetes, participating in support groups, and developing a routine can empower you to navigate the challenges of this journey. Acknowledging that you are taking positive steps can foster resilience and a more optimistic outlook.

Furthermore, successful management of diabetes often involves lifestyle changes that benefit overall health, such as adopting a balanced diet and incorporating regular physical activity. These lifestyle improvements can lead to weight loss, enhanced cardiovascular health, and better emotional well-being. For many, the process of learning to cook healthier

meals or finding enjoyable ways to exercise becomes a rewarding journey in itself.

In summary, the importance of managing diabetes after 50 extends far beyond merely controlling blood sugar levels. It encompasses the reduction of serious health risks, the enhancement of daily life, and the cultivation of emotional resilience. By prioritizing diabetes management, you empower yourself to thrive during this vibrant stage of life, ensuring that health challenges do not overshadow the joys and experiences that come with aging. Embracing this responsibility is not just about survival; it's about living well and fully in your golden years.

Differences in Diabetes: Older Adults vs. Younger Individuals

Diabetes affects individuals of all ages, but the way it manifests and is managed can differ significantly between older adults and younger individuals. Understanding these differences is crucial for tailoring effective management strategies and ensuring optimal health outcomes.

1. Pathophysiological Differences

In younger individuals, diabetes is often associated with lifestyle factors, such as obesity and inactivity, particularly in the case of Type 2 diabetes. Younger adults tend to have a more robust insulin response and are generally more physically active, which can help mitigate the effects of insulin resistance. In contrast, older adults may experience a gradual decline in insulin sensitivity due to age-related physiological changes, such as decreased muscle mass and altered hormonal regulation. This decline can lead to more pronounced blood sugar fluctuations and increased difficulty in managing the condition.

2. Symptoms and Complications

The symptoms of diabetes can also vary by age. Younger individuals may experience more acute symptoms, such as increased thirst, frequent urination, and unexplained weight loss. These symptoms often prompt an earlier diagnosis. Conversely, older adults might have more subtle or atypical symptoms, such as fatigue or blurred vision, which can be mistakenly attributed to aging rather than diabetes. Additionally, older adults are at greater risk for diabetes-related complications, such as cardiovascular disease, neuropathy, and cognitive decline, making proactive management even more critical.

3. Medication Considerations

Younger individuals may be more likely to manage their diabetes through lifestyle changes and oral medications. In contrast, older adults often have multiple health conditions, which can complicate diabetes management. They might require a combination of medications, including insulin, to achieve optimal blood sugar control. Furthermore, age-related changes in metabolism and kidney function can affect how medications are absorbed and eliminated, necessitating careful monitoring and adjustments.

4. Psychosocial Factors

The psychosocial aspects of living with diabetes can differ dramatically between age groups. Younger individuals may face unique challenges, such as balancing diabetes management with work, family responsibilities, and social activities. They might struggle with the fear of long-term complications, which can lead to anxiety. Older adults, on the other hand, may experience feelings of isolation or depression, particularly if they have limited mobility or social support. These emotional factors can significantly impact adherence to treatment and lifestyle modifications.

5. Lifestyle and Support Systems

Younger individuals may have more access to technology and resources that facilitate diabetes management, such as continuous glucose monitors and mobile health apps. These tools can help with real-time tracking of blood sugar levels and provide reminders for medication. Older adults, however, may face barriers such as lack of technological proficiency or limited access to healthcare resources. Additionally, the social networks of older adults might be different, with varying levels of family support and community resources available for managing diabetes.

6. Approach to Prevention and Education

Education about diabetes management is essential for all age groups, but the approach may differ. Younger individuals might benefit from strategies that emphasize lifestyle changes and long-term planning for health. For older adults, education should focus on recognizing symptoms, understanding medication regimens, and navigating the healthcare system. Tailoring educational resources to fit the needs and preferences of different age groups can enhance their effectiveness and improve health outcomes.

Recognizing the differences in diabetes management between older adults and younger individuals is crucial for providing appropriate care. By understanding these distinctions, we can better tailor interventions, support systems, and educational resources to help each group effectively manage their diabetes and improve their overall quality of life.

Basics of Diabetes After 50

Understanding the basics of diabetes is essential for effectively managing the condition, especially as we age. Diabetes is a chronic disease characterized by high blood sugar levels resulting from the body's inability to produce or effectively use insulin. As we enter our 50s and beyond, the risk of developing diabetes increases due to various factors, including hormonal changes, decreased physical activity, and lifestyle habits.

1. Types of Diabetes

There are primarily two types of diabetes that affect adults:

- **Type 1 Diabetes:** This autoimmune condition typically develops earlier in life and occurs when the pancreas produces little to no insulin. While it's less common in older adults, some may develop late-onset Type 1 diabetes.

- **Type 2 Diabetes:** This is the most prevalent form,

especially in older adults. It often develops due to insulin resistance, where the body's cells do not respond effectively to insulin. Over time, the pancreas may not produce enough insulin to maintain normal blood sugar levels. Factors contributing to Type 2 diabetes include obesity, sedentary lifestyle, genetics, and age.

2. Symptoms of Diabetes

The symptoms of diabetes can vary, and some may be more pronounced in older adults. Common symptoms include:

- Increased thirst and frequent urination
- Fatigue or weakness
- Blurred vision
- Slow healing of wounds
- Unexplained weight loss (more common in Type 1)

It's important to note that some older adults may experience atypical symptoms, such as increased confusion or mood changes, which can complicate diagnosis.

3. Diagnosis

Diagnosing diabetes typically involves blood tests that measure blood sugar levels. Common methods include:

- **Fasting Blood Sugar Test:** Measures blood sugar after an overnight fast. A level of 126 mg/dL (7.0 mmol/L) or higher indicates diabetes.

- **Oral Glucose Tolerance Test (OGTT):** Measures blood sugar before and two hours after consuming a sugary drink. A two-hour level of 200 mg/dL (11.1 mmol/L) or higher indicates diabetes.

- **Hemoglobin A1c Test:** Reflects average blood sugar levels over the past two to three months. An A1c level of 6.5% or higher indicates diabetes.

Regular screenings are crucial for early detection, especially for those with risk factors such as obesity, family history, or a sedentary lifestyle.

4. Management Goals

Effective diabetes management aims to maintain blood sugar levels within a target range, typically between 80-130 mg/dL (4.4-7.2 mmol/L) before meals and less than 180 mg/dL (10.0 mmol/L) two hours after eating. Achieving these goals can help prevent complications such as heart disease, kidney damage, and neuropathy.

5. Lifestyle Factors

Managing diabetes after 50 involves a holistic approach that includes:

- **Healthy Eating:** Focusing on a balanced diet rich in whole grains, lean proteins, healthy fats, fruits, and vegetables. Understanding carbohydrate counting and portion control is vital for regulating blood sugar.

- **Physical Activity:** Regular exercise helps improve insulin sensitivity, manage weight, and enhance overall well-being. Aim for at least 150 minutes of moderate-intensity aerobic activity each week, along with strength training exercises.

- **Monitoring Blood Sugar:** Regular self-monitoring helps you understand how different foods and activities affect your blood sugar levels. Keeping a log can assist in making informed decisions about diet and medication.

- **Medication Management:** Many older adults may require oral medications or insulin therapy to help control blood sugar levels. It's important to follow prescribed regimens and discuss any concerns with healthcare providers.

6. Regular Check-ups

Routine medical check-ups are essential for monitoring diabetes management and overall health. Regular visits to healthcare professionals can help catch potential complications early and adjust treatment plans as needed.

By grasping these fundamental aspects of diabetes, older adults can take proactive steps toward managing their health effectively. Awareness of the types, symptoms, diagnosis, and management strategies equips individuals with the knowledge needed to navigate this condition confidently and maintain a fulfilling lifestyle.

Nutritional Needs for Those Over 50

As we age, our nutritional needs evolve, particularly for those managing diabetes. Meeting these needs is crucial for maintaining health, managing blood sugar levels, and preventing complications. Understanding the specific dietary requirements for individuals over

50 can significantly enhance overall well-being.

✓ Balanced Diet

A well-balanced diet is fundamental. It's essential to incorporate a variety of food groups, including:

- Fruits and Vegetables: Aim for at least five servings a day. These provide essential vitamins, minerals, and antioxidants while being low in calories and high in fiber, which aids in blood sugar control.

- Whole Grains: Opt for whole grains such as brown rice, quinoa, and whole-wheat bread. These are rich in fiber, helping to slow down glucose absorption and maintain stable blood sugar levels.

- Lean Proteins: Include sources of lean protein like chicken, turkey, fish, legumes, and low-fat dairy. Protein is essential for muscle maintenance, especially as muscle mass tends to decrease with age.

- Healthy Fats: Incorporate healthy fats from sources like avocados, nuts, seeds, and olive oil. These fats are beneficial for heart health and can help reduce inflammation.

✓ Carbohydrate Management

Carbohydrates have the most significant impact on blood sugar levels, making their management essential for those with diabetes. Choosing complex carbohydrates over simple sugars is crucial. Complex carbs, such as whole grains and legumes, provide sustained energy and are digested more slowly, preventing spikes in blood sugar.

✓ Fiber Intake

Increasing fiber intake is particularly beneficial for older adults. Fiber not only aids digestion and prevents constipation but also helps regulate blood sugar levels. Aim for at least 25-30 grams of fiber daily, incorporating foods like fruits, vegetables, whole grains, and legumes.

✓ Hydration

Staying hydrated is often overlooked but essential, especially for older adults who may experience a decreased sense of thirst. Aim to drink plenty of water throughout the day, and consider including hydrating foods like soups and fruits. Adequate hydration supports overall health and can help prevent urinary tract infections and constipation.

✓ Vitamins and Minerals

Certain vitamins and minerals become increasingly important as we age:

- Calcium and Vitamin D: These are crucial for maintaining bone health, which can deteriorate with age. Sources include dairy, fortified plant-based milks, and leafy greens. Sunlight exposure also helps the body produce vitamin D.

- B Vitamins: B vitamins, particularly B12, are vital for energy production and nerve function. Older adults may have a harder time absorbing B12, so considering fortified foods or supplements can be beneficial.

- Magnesium: This mineral is important for blood sugar control and is found in foods like nuts, seeds, and whole grains.

✓ Portion Control

As metabolism slows with age, portion control becomes increasingly important to manage weight and blood sugar levels. Being mindful of serving sizes can help prevent overeating, especially when consuming higher-calorie foods.

✓ Meal Timing

Regular meal timing can help stabilize blood sugar levels. Aim for consistent meal times and consider incorporating healthy snacks between meals to prevent blood sugar dips.

Addressing these nutritional needs allows individuals over 50 to manage diabetes more effectively. A well-rounded diet not only supports blood sugar control but also enhances overall vitality, promoting a more active and fulfilling lifestyle.

Tips and Strategies for Managing Diabetes

Managing diabetes, especially after 50, requires a proactive approach that combines lifestyle changes, education, and support. Here are practical tips and strategies to help individuals effectively manage their condition and enhance their quality of life.

1. Educate Yourself
Knowledge is power when it comes to diabetes management. Understanding how diabetes affects the body, the role of insulin, and the impact of various foods can help in making informed decisions. Consider attending diabetes education programs or workshops to gain insights and tips from healthcare professionals.

2. Monitor Blood Sugar Regularly
Regular monitoring of blood sugar levels is crucial for effective management. Keeping track of your numbers helps identify patterns related to food, activity, and medication. Use a glucose meter or continuous glucose monitor (CGM) to stay informed and make adjustments as needed.

3. Create a Meal Plan
Developing a structured meal plan can help manage blood sugar levels. Include a variety of foods, focusing on whole grains, lean proteins, healthy fats, and plenty of fruits and vegetables. Meal prepping can simplify the process and reduce the temptation to opt for unhealthy choices.

4. Practice Portion Control
Being mindful of portion sizes can prevent overeating and help maintain stable blood sugar levels. Use smaller plates, measure servings, and pay attention to hunger cues. Familiarizing yourself with standard serving sizes can aid in making better choices.

5. Stay Active
Regular physical activity plays a vital role in diabetes management. Aim for at least 150 minutes of moderate-intensity aerobic exercise each week, along with strength training exercises on two or more days. Activities like walking, swimming, and cycling can improve insulin sensitivity and overall health.

6. Manage Stress
Stress can negatively impact blood sugar levels, so finding effective ways to manage stress is essential. Consider practices such as yoga, meditation, deep breathing exercises, or hobbies that bring joy. Regular physical activity can also be a great stress reliever.

7. Stay Hydrated
Drinking enough water is important for overall health and can help with blood sugar control. Aim to drink at least eight glasses of water a day. Herbal teas and infused water can be good alternatives to sugary drinks.

8. Keep Healthy Snacks on Hand
Having healthy snacks readily available can prevent blood sugar dips and help avoid unhealthy eating. Consider options like nuts, yogurt, fresh fruits, or raw vegetables. These snacks provide nutrients while keeping blood sugar levels stable.

9. Communicate with Healthcare Providers
Regular communication with healthcare professionals is key to effective diabetes management. Schedule routine check-ups, discuss any concerns, and adjust medications as needed. Building a supportive healthcare team can provide valuable resources and encouragement.

10. Plan for Dining Out
Eating out can be challenging, but with some planning, it can be manageable. Research restaurant menus in advance, choose dishes that are grilled, baked, or steamed, and ask for dressings or sauces on the side. Portion control and mindful eating remain essential when dining out.

11. Involve Family and Friends
Having a support system can make a significant difference in managing diabetes. Involve family and friends in your journey by sharing your goals and challenges. Their understanding and encouragement can provide motivation and accountability.

12. Stay Flexible
Diabetes management is not a one-size-fits-all approach. Be willing to adjust your strategies as needed. What works one day may not work the next, and that's okay. Flexibility allows for better adaptation to changing circumstances, whether related to health, lifestyle, or personal preferences.

Implementing these tips and strategies can empower individuals over 50 to take charge of their diabetes management. With a combination of education, planning, and support, it's possible to lead a fulfilling life while effectively managing the condition.

Meal Plan and Shopping List

Creating a meal plan and shopping list is essential for effective diabetes management, especially for individuals over 50. A structured approach simplifies meal preparation and helps maintain stable blood sugar levels. Here's how to develop a meal plan and create an efficient shopping list.

Meal Planning
- **Set Goals:** Begin by determining your dietary objectives, such as managing blood sugar levels, maintaining a healthy weight, and ensuring nutritional balance. Consider any specific dietary restrictions or preferences.

- **Choose a Planning Method:** Decide whether you prefer digital tools, such as apps or spreadsheets, or traditional methods like a notebook. Select the method that works best for you.

- **Plan Balanced Meals:** Aim for a variety of meals that include lean proteins, whole grains, healthy fats, and plenty of fruits and vegetables. Explore different cooking methods, such as grilling, baking, or steaming, to keep meals interesting.

- **Create a Weekly Menu:** Outline a weekly menu that encompasses breakfast, lunch, dinner, and snacks. Keep your schedule in mind, planning for busier days and incorporating leftovers for convenience.

- **Consider Portion Sizes:** When planning meals, pay attention to portion sizes to help regulate blood sugar levels. Familiarizing yourself with appropriate serving sizes using measuring cups or a food scale can be helpful.

- **Prepare for Flexibility:** Allow room for flexibility in your meal plan to accommodate unexpected events or cravings. Having a few quick and healthy meal options readily available can assist in this regard.

- **Review and Adjust:** At the end of each week, review your meal plan to assess what worked well and what didn't, making adjustments for the following week as needed.

Creating a Shopping List
- **Inventory Your Pantry and Fridge:** Before making a shopping list, check your pantry and refrigerator for items you already have. This helps avoid duplicates and reduces waste.

- **Categorize Your List:** Organize your shopping list by food categories, such as fruits, vegetables, proteins, grains, and dairy. This makes shopping more efficient and ensures you don't forget any essentials.

- **Include Specific Items:** For each category, list specific items needed for your meal plan. Choose fresh, seasonal produce whenever possible and opt for whole grains over processed options.

- **Plan for Snacks:** Include healthy snacks on your list. Choose options that are easy to grab, such as nuts, yogurt, or cut-up vegetables.

- **Check for Labels:** When shopping, pay attention to nutrition labels, focusing on items with lower added sugars, healthier fats, and higher fiber content. This is particularly important for packaged foods.

- ◆ **Stick to Your List:** Aim to adhere closely to your shopping list to avoid impulse purchases, especially those that may not align with your dietary goals.

- ◆ **Shop Mindfully:** Consider shopping when you're not hungry to reduce the temptation to buy unhealthy foods. Taking your time to read labels fosters informed choices.

A systematic approach to meal planning and shopping empowers individuals to take control of their dietary choices, making it easier to manage diabetes while enjoying a variety of nutritious foods. This organized strategy enhances overall meal enjoyment and satisfaction.

Tips for Dining Out

Dining out can be enjoyable and manageable for those managing diabetes, especially after 50. With a few strategies, it's possible to make informed choices that align with your dietary goals. Here are some practical tips for navigating restaurant meals:

1. Research the Menu Ahead of Time
Before heading out, review the restaurant's menu online. Look for healthier options and familiarize yourself with dishes that fit your dietary needs. This preparation can help you make confident choices once you're there.

2. Choose Restaurants Wisely
Opt for restaurants that offer a variety of healthy options, including salads, grilled meats, and whole grains. Some places even provide nutritional information, which can assist in making informed choices.

3. Watch Portion Sizes
Restaurant portions can be significantly larger than what you would typically serve at home. Consider sharing an entrée with someone or asking for a half portion. If neither is an option, request a takeaway container when your meal arrives and set aside part of it for later.

4. Ask for Modifications
Don't hesitate to ask the server for modifications to your meal. Request dressings or sauces on the side, choose steamed vegetables instead of fries, or ask for grilled instead of fried options. Most restaurants are willing to accommodate reasonable requests.

5. Be Mindful of Bread and Appetizers
Bread baskets and appetizers can be tempting but may contribute unnecessary carbs. Consider skipping the bread or sharing appetizers with the table. If you choose to indulge, limit your portion and be mindful of what's to come.

6. Choose Wisely for Drinks
Beverages can add hidden sugars and calories. Opt for water, sparkling water, or unsweetened tea instead of sugary sodas or alcoholic drinks. If you do choose alcohol, consider light options and limit consumption.

7. Plan for Snacks or Side Dishes
If you're dining out at a time that falls between meals, plan accordingly. Bring a healthy snack to enjoy beforehand or choose a side dish that is filling yet nutritious, such as a salad with lean protein.

8. Listen to Your Body
Pay attention to your hunger and fullness cues. Eat slowly and enjoy each bite, which can help you recognize when you're satisfied. This practice can prevent overeating and promote better digestion.

9. Stay Consistent with Your Meal Timing
Try to maintain your regular meal timing, even when dining out. If you usually have dinner at 6 PM, aim for that time to keep your blood sugar levels stable. This consistency helps manage cravings and keeps you on track.

10. Reflect on Your Experience
After dining out, take a moment to reflect on what choices worked well and what you might change next time. Learning from each experience can enhance your confidence in making healthy dining decisions.

With these strategies, dining out can remain a pleasurable experience without compromising health. Enjoying meals out while successfully managing diabetes is entirely achievable with the right approach.

CHAPTER 2: BREAKFAST

Pumpkin Pancakes

PREP TIME: 10 MINUTES, **COOK TIME:** 10 MINUTES, **SERVES:** 2

INGREDIENTS:
- Nonstick cooking spray
- 4 eggs
- 1 cup fine ground almond flour
- ½ cup pumpkin puree
- 2 tsps. liquid stevia
- 1 tsp. baking powder
- ½ tsp. cinnamon

DIRECTIONS:
1. Mix all ingredients in a medium bowl and whisk until thoroughly combined.
2. Spray a small nonstick skillet with cooking spray and place over med-high heat.
3. Pour about ¼-⅓ cup batter into skillet, spreading out evenly. Cook until brown on the bottom. Flip and repeat with the other side.
4. Serve with a little sugar-free syrup if desired.

Nutrition Info per Serving:
Calories: 404, Protein: 22 g, Fat: 21 g, Carbohydrates: 17 g, Fiber: 4 g, Sugar: 7 g, Sodium: 350 mg

---

Chia Pudding with Fruits

PREP TIME: 5 MINUTES, **COOK TIME:** 0 MINUTES, **SERVES:** 2

INGREDIENTS:
- 7 ounces (198 g) light coconut milk
- ¼ cup chia seeds
- 3 to 4 drops liquid stevia
- 1 clementine
- 1 kiwi
- Shredded coconut (unsweetened)

DIRECTIONS:
1. Start by taking a mixing bowl and adding in the light coconut milk. Add in the liquid stevia to sweeten the milk. Mix well.
2. Add the chia seeds to the milk and whisk until well-combined. Set aside.
3. Peel the clementine and carefully remove the skin from the wedges. Set aside.
4. Also, peel the kiwi and dice it into small pieces.
5. Take a glass jar and assemble the pudding. For this, place the fruits at the bottom of the jar; then add a dollop of chia pudding. Now spread the fruits and then add another layer of chia pudding.
6. Finish by garnishing with the remaining fruits and shredded coconut.

Nutrition Info per Serving:
Calories: 340, Protein: 6 g, Fat: 24 g, Carbohydrates: 32 g, Fiber: 11 g, Sugar: 10 g, Sodium: 30 mg

Poached Eggs & Grits

PREP TIME: 1 MINUTE, **COOK TIME:** 10 MINUTES, **SERVES:** 4

INGREDIENTS:
- 4 eggs, poached
- 3 cups skim milk
- 1 cup grits
- ¼ cup low-fat Colby cheese, grated
- 2 tsp. reduced fat Parmesan cheese, grated

DIRECTIONS:
1. In a large microwavable bowl, stir together the grits and most of the milk, save a little to stir in later. Cook for 8-10 minutes, stirring every couple of minutes.
2. Meanwhile, poach the eggs in a large pot of boiling water.
3. When grits are done, stir in the Colby cheese and Parmesan cheese until melted and smooth. If they seem too stiff, add the remaining milk.
4. Ladle into 4 bowls and top each with a poached egg, serve.

Nutrition Info per Serving:
Calories: 270, Protein: 16 g, Fat: 9 g, Carbohydrates: 28 g, Fiber: 1 g, Sugar: 4 g, Sodium: 330 mg

Healthy Buckwheat Crêpes

PREP TIME: 20 MINUTES, **COOK TIME:** 20 MINUTES, **SERVES:** 5

INGREDIENTS:
- 1 tsp. extra-virgin olive oil, plus more for the skillet
- 3 eggs
- 1½ cups skim milk
- 1 cup sliced strawberries
- 1 cup blueberries
- 1 cup buckwheat flour
- ½ cup whole-wheat flour
- ½ cup 2 percent plain Greek yogurt

DIRECTIONS:
1. In a large bowl, whisk together the milk, eggs, and 1 tsp. of oil until well combined.
2. Into a medium bowl, sift together the buckwheat and whole-wheat flours. Add the dry ingredients to the wet ingredients and whisk until well combined and very smooth.
3. Allow the batter to rest for at least 2 hours before cooking.
4. Place a large skillet or crêpe pan over medium-high heat and lightly coat the bottom with oil.
5. Pour about ¼ cup of batter into the skillet. Swirl the pan until the batter completely coats the bottom.
6. Cook the crêpe for about 1 minute, then flip it over. Cook the other side of the crêpe for another minute, until lightly browned. Transfer the cooked crêpe to a plate and cover with a clean dish towel to keep warm.
7. Repeat until the batter is used up; you should have about 10 crêpes.
8. Spoon 1 tbsp. of yogurt onto each crêpe and place two crêpes on each plate.
9. Top with berries and serve.

Nutrition Info per Serving:
Calories: 315, Protein: 12 g, Fat: 7 g, Carbohydrates: 55 g, Fiber: 6 g, Sugar: 8 g, Sodium: 120 mg

Chapter 2: Breakfast / 11

Ratatouille Egg Bake

PREP TIME: 20 MINUTES, **COOK TIME:** 50 MINUTES, **SERVES:** 4

INGREDIENTS:
- 2 tsps. extra-virgin olive oil
- 4 large eggs
- 1 green zucchini, diced
- 1 yellow zucchini, diced
- 1 red bell pepper, seeded and diced
- 3 tomatoes, seeded and chopped
- ½ sweet onion, finely chopped
- ½ small eggplant, peeled and diced
- 2 tsps. minced garlic
- 1 tbsp. chopped fresh oregano
- 1 tbsp. chopped fresh basil
- Pinch red pepper flakes
- Sea salt and freshly ground black pepper, to taste

DIRECTIONS:
1. Preheat the oven to 350ºF (180ºC).
2. Place a large ovenproof skillet over medium heat and add the olive oil.
3. Sauté the onion and garlic until softened and translucent, about 3 minutes. Stir in the eggplant and sauté for about 10 minutes, stirring occasionally. Stir in the zucchinis and red pepper and sauté for 5 minutes.
4. Reduce the heat to low and cover. Cook until the vegetables are soft, about 15 minutes.
5. Stir in the tomatoes, oregano, basil, and red pepper flakes, and cook for 10 minutes more. Season the ratatouille with salt and pepper.
6. Use a spoon to create four wells in the mixture. Crack an egg into each well.
7. Place the skillet in the oven and bake until the eggs are firm, about 5 minutes.
8. Remove from the oven. Serve the eggs with a generous scoop of vegetables.

Nutrition Info per Serving:
Calories: 200, Protein: 10 g, Fat: 12 g, Carbohydrates: 15 g, Fiber: 5 g, Sugar: 5 g, Sodium: 289 mg

....

Cheese Mushroom Frittata

PREP TIME: 10 MINUTES, **COOK TIME:** 15 MINUTES, **SERVES:** 4

INGREDIENTS:
- 2 tsps. extra-virgin olive oil
- 8 large eggs
- ½ cup skim milk
- 2 cups sliced wild mushrooms (cremini, oyster, shiitake, portobello, etc.)
- ½ cup low-fat goat cheese, crumbled
- ¼ tsp. ground nutmeg
- Sea salt and freshly ground black pepper, to taste
- ½ red onion, chopped
- 1 tsp. minced garlic

DIRECTIONS:
1. Preheat the broiler.
2. In a medium bowl, whisk together the eggs, milk, and nutmeg until well combined. Season the egg mixture lightly with salt and pepper and set it aside.
3. Place an ovenproof skillet over medium heat and add the oil, coating the bottom completely by tilting the pan.
4. Sauté the mushrooms, onion, and garlic until translucent, about 7 minutes.
5. Pour the egg mixture into the skillet and cook until the bottom of the frittata is set, lifting the edges of the cooked egg to allow the uncooked egg to seep under.
6. Place the skillet under the broiler until the top is set, about 1 minute.
7. Sprinkle the goat cheese on the frittata and broil until the cheese is melted, about 1 minute more.
8. Remove from the oven. Cut into 4 wedges to serve.

Nutrition Info per Serving:
Calories: 210, Protein: 15 g, Fat: 15 g, Carbohydrates: 6 g, Fiber: 1 g, Sugar: 1 g, Sodium: 224 mg

Walnut and Oat Granola

PREP TIME: 10 MINUTES, **COOK TIME:** 30 MINUTES, **SERVES:** 16

INGREDIENTS:
- 4 cups rolled oats
- 1 cup walnut pieces
- ½ cup pepitas
- ½ cup dried cherries
- ½ cup coconut oil, melted
- ½ cup unsweetened applesauce
- ¼ tsp. salt
- 1 tsp. ground cinnamon
- 1 tsp. ground ginger
- 1 tsp. vanilla extract

DIRECTIONS:
1. Preheat the oven to 350ºF (180ºC). Line a baking sheet with parchment paper.
2. In a large bowl, toss the oats, walnuts, pepitas, salt, cinnamon, and ginger.
3. In a large measuring cup, combine the coconut oil, applesauce, and vanilla. Pour over the dry mixture and mix well.
4. Transfer the mixture to the prepared baking sheet. Bake for 30 minutes, stirring about halfway through. Remove from the oven and let the granola sit undisturbed until completely cool. Break the granola into pieces, and stir in the dried cherries.
5. Transfer to an airtight container, and store at room temperature for up to 2 weeks.

Nutrition Info per Serving:
Calories: 195, Protein: 4 g, Fat: 9 g, Carbohydrates: 21 g, Fiber: 3 g, Sugar: 3 g, Sodium: 50 mg

Peanut Butter Waffles

PREP TIME: 5 MINUTES, **COOK TIME:** 10 MINUTES, **SERVES:** 4

INGREDIENTS:
- Nonstick cooking spray
- 4 eggs
- ⅔ cup low-fat peanut butter
- ½ cup low fat cream cheese
- ½ cup unsweetened almond milk
- 2 tbsps. almond butter
- 2 tsp. stevia
- 1 tsp. baking powder

DIRECTIONS:
1. Lightly spray waffle iron with cooking spray and preheat.
2. In a medium glass bowl, place peanut butter, almond butter, and cream cheese. Microwave 30 seconds and stir to combine.
3. Stir in the unsweetened almond milk, baking powder, and stevia and mix until all the ingredients are combined. Stir in eggs and mix well.
4. Ladle into waffle iron and cook until golden brown and crisp on the outside. Serve.

Nutrition Info per Serving:
Calories: 347, Protein: 21 g, Fat: 20 g, Carbohydrates: 15 g, Fiber: 2 g, Sugar: 2 g, Sodium: 218 mg

Chapter 2: Breakfast / 13

Coconut and Blueberry Oatmeal

🕐 **PREP TIME:** 10 MINUTES, **COOK TIME:** 35 MINUTES, **SERVES:** 6

INGREDIENTS:

- ¼ cup melted coconut oil, plus extra for greasing the baking dish
- 1 egg
- 2 cups fresh blueberries
- 2 cups rolled oats
- ¼ cup shredded unsweetened coconut
- 1 tsp. baking powder
- ½ tsp. ground cinnamon
- ¼ tsp. sea salt
- 2 cups skim milk
- 1 tsp. pure vanilla extract
- ⅛ cup chopped pecans, for garnish
- 1 tsp. chopped fresh mint leaves, for garnish

DIRECTIONS:

1. Preheat the oven to 350ºF (180ºC).
2. Lightly oil a baking dish and set it aside.
3. In a medium bowl, stir together the oats, coconut, baking powder, cinnamon, and salt.
4. In a small bowl, whisk together the milk, oil, egg, and vanilla until well blended.
5. Layer half the dry ingredients in the baking dish, top with half the berries, then spoon the remaining half of the dry ingredients and the rest of the berries on top.
6. Pour the wet ingredients evenly into the baking dish. Tap it lightly on the counter to disperse the wet ingredients throughout.
7. Bake the casserole, uncovered, until the oats are tender, about 35 minutes.
8. Serve immediately, topped with the pecans and mint.

Nutrition Info per Serving:
Calories: 190, Protein: 5 g, Fat: 8 g, Carbohydrates: 29 g, Fiber: 3 g, Sugar: 6 g, Sodium: 80 mg

....

Spinach & Tomato Egg Muffins

🕐 **PREP TIME:** 5 MINUTES, **COOK TIME:** 25 MINUTES, **SERVES:** 6

INGREDIENTS:

- Nonstick cooking spray
- 6 eggs
- 1 avocado, sliced
- ½ cup fresh spinach, diced
- ⅓ cup tomatoes, diced
- ⅓ cup reduced-fat cheddar cheese, grated
- ¼ cup almond milk, unsweetened
- 2 green onions, sliced
- Salt and pepper

DIRECTIONS:

1. Heat oven to 350ºF (180ºC). Spray a muffin pan with cooking spray.
2. In a large bowl, beat together eggs, milk, and salt and pepper to taste.
3. Add remaining ingredients and mix well.
4. Divide evenly between 6 muffin cups. Bake for 20-25 minutes or until egg is set in the middle.
5. Remove from oven let cool for 5 minutes. Serve topped with sliced avocado.

Nutrition Info per Serving:
Calories: 160, Protein: 10 g, Fat: 10 g, Carbohydrates: 8 g, Fiber: 2 g, Sugar: 1 g, Sodium: 220 mg

CHAPTER 3: FISH AND SEAFOOD

Parchment-Paper Halibut with Lemon

PREP TIME: 15 MINUTES, **COOK TIME:** 15 MINUTES, **SERVES:** 4

INGREDIENTS:
- 4 tsps. extra-virgin olive oil
- 4 (5-ounce, 142g) halibut fillets (about 1 inch thick)
- ½ cup zucchini, diced small
- 1 lemon, sliced into ⅛-inch-thick rounds
- 8 sprigs of thyme
- 1 shallot, minced
- ¼ tsp. kosher salt
- ⅛ tsp. freshly ground black pepper

DIRECTIONS:
1. Preheat the oven to 450°F(235°C). Combine the zucchini and shallots in a medium bowl.
2. Cut 4 (15-by-24-inch) pieces of parchment paper. Fold each sheet in half horizontally. Draw a large half heart on one side of each folded sheet, with the fold along the center of the heart. Cut out the heart, open the parchment, and lay it flat.
3. Place a fillet near the center of each parchment heart. Drizzle 1 tsp. olive oil on each fillet. Sprinkle with salt and pepper. Top each fillet with lemon slices and 2 sprigs of thyme. Sprinkle each fillet with one-quarter of the zucchini and shallot mixture. Fold the parchment over.
4. Starting at the top, fold the edges of the parchment over, and continue all the way around to make a packet. Twist the end tightly to secure.
5. Arrange the 4 packets on a baking sheet. Bake for about 15 minutes. Place on plates, cut open. Serve immediately.

Nutrition Info per Serving:
Calories: 240, Protein: 27 g, Fat: 8 g, Carbohydrates: 6 g, Fiber: 1 g, Sugar: 1 g

Cod with Asparagus

PREP TIME: 15 MINUTES, **COOK TIME:** 11 MINUTES, **SERVES:** 2

INGREDIENTS:
- 1 tbsp. olive oil
- 2 (6-ounces) boneless cod fillets
- 1 bunch asparagus
- 2 tbsps. fresh parsley, roughly chopped
- 2 tbsps. fresh dill, roughly chopped
- 1 tsp. dried basil
- 1½ tbsps. fresh lemon juice
- Salt and black pepper, to taste

DIRECTIONS:
1. Preheat the Air fryer to 400ºF (204ºC) and grease an Air fryer basket.
2. Mix lemon juice, oil, parsley, dill, basil, salt, and black pepper in a small bowl.
3. Combine the cod and ¾ of the oil mixture in another bowl.
4. Coat asparagus with remaining oil mixture and transfer to the Air fryer basket.
5. Roast for about 3 minutes and arrange cod fillets on top of asparagus.
6. Roast for about 8 minutes and dish out in serving plates.

Nutrition Info per Serving:
Calories: 238, Protein: 32 g, Fat: 9 g, Carbohydrates: 8 g, Fiber: 4 g, Sugar: 2 g, Sodium: 220 mg

Chapter 3: Fish and Seafood / 15

Mahi Mahi with Green Beans

🕐 **PREP TIME:** 15 MINUTES, **COOK TIME:** 12 MINUTES, **SERVES:** 4

INGREDIENTS:
- 1 tbsp. avocado oil
- 5 cups green beans
- 2 tbsps. fresh dill, chopped
- 1 tbsp. olive oil
- 4 (6-ounces) Mahi Mahi fillets
- 2 garlic cloves, minced
- 2 tbsps. fresh lemon juice
- Salt, as required

DIRECTIONS:
1. Preheat the Air fryer to 375ºF (191ºC) and grease an Air fryer basket.
2. Mix the green beans, avocado oil and salt in a large bowl.
3. Arrange green beans into the Air fryer basket and air fry for about 6 minutes.
4. Combine garlic, dill, lemon juice, salt and olive oil in a bowl.
5. Coat Mahi Mahi in this garlic mixture and place on the top of green beans.
6. Air fry for 6 more minutes and dish out to serve warm.

Nutrition Info per Serving:
Calories: 320, Protein: 30 g, Fat: 18 g, Carbohydrates: 10 g, Fiber: 4 g, Sugar: 2 g, Sodium: 207 mg

---

Spicy Shrimp Kebabs

🕐 **PREP TIME:** 15 MINUTES, **COOK TIME:** 10 MINUTES, **SERVES:** 2

INGREDIENTS:
- ¾ pound shrimp, peeled and deveined
- Wooden skewers, presoaked
- 2 tbsps. fresh lemon juice
- 1 tbsp. fresh cilantro, chopped
- 1 tsp. garlic, minced
- ½ tsp. paprika
- ½ tsp. ground cumin
- Salt and ground black pepper, as required

DIRECTIONS:
1. Preheat the Air fryer to 350ºF (177ºC) and grease an Air fryer basket.
2. Mix lemon juice, cumin, garlic, and paprika in a bowl.
3. Stir in the shrimp and mix to coat well. Season with salt and pepper to taste.
4. Thread the shrimp onto presoaked wooden skewers and transfer to the Air fryer basket.
5. Roast for about 10 minutes, flipping once in between.
6. Dish out the mixture onto serving plates and serve garnished with fresh cilantro.

Nutrition Info per Serving:
Calories: 189, Protein: 33 g, Fat: 4 g, Carbohydrates: 7 g, Fiber: 1 g, Sugar: 1 g, Sodium: 475 mg

Easy Mediterranean Scallops

PREP TIME: 5 MINUTES, **COOK TIME:** 12 TO 15 MINUTES, **SERVES:** 4

INGREDIENTS:
- 3 tbsps. extra-virgin olive oil, divided
- 12 scallops
- ¼ cup fresh thyme leaves
- ¼ cup fresh basil leaves
- 1 garlic clove, minced
- 1 tbsp. fresh lemon juice
- 1 tbsp. fresh rosemary leaves
- 1 tbsp. chopped fresh sage
- 2 tsps. freshly ground black pepper
- 4 lemon wedges (optional)

DIRECTIONS:
1. In a food processor or blender, combine the basil, thyme, rosemary, sage, pepper, lemon juice, and 1½ tbsps. of oil. Pulse until mixed. The herbs should still be visible.
2. In a large skillet, heat the remaining 1½ tbsps. of oil over medium-high heat. Add the garlic and cook, stirring rapidly for 30 seconds. Working in batches, sear the scallops on each side, for 2 to 3 minutes per side. Remove from the skillet and top with the herbed oil. Place 3 herb-topped scallops in each of 4 storage containers.
3. To serve, after reheating the scallops, place a lemon wedge on the side (if using).

Nutrition Info per Serving:
Calories: 158, Protein: 12 g, Fat: 11 g, Carbohydrates: 2 g, Fiber: 1 g, Sugar: 0 g, Sodium: 235 mg

Haddock Tacos with Cabbage

PREP TIME: 10 MINUTES, **COOK TIME:** 5 MINUTES, **SERVES:** 2

INGREDIENTS:
- 3 tsps. extra-virgin olive oil
- 8 ounces (227 g) skinless haddock fillets, cut into 1-inch chunks
- 2 cups angel hair cabbage
- ½ avocado, chopped
- 2 tbsps. fresh lime juice
- 1 tsp. ground cumin
- ½ tsp. chili powder
- ⅛ tsp. salt
- ⅛ tsp. freshly ground black pepper
- 2 (6-inch) whole-wheat tortillas, warmed
- Fresh cilantro, for serving

DIRECTIONS:
1. Mix the chili powder, cumin, salt, and pepper in a small bowl. Add the haddock and toss to coat.
2. In a separate small bowl, mix together the cabbage, lime juice, avocado, and 1 tsp. olive oil.
3. Heat the remaining olive oil in a medium skillet over medium-high heat. Add the haddock and cook for 4 to 5 minutes, turning, until the fish is just opaque and flakes easily with a fork.
4. Portion the fish between the warmed tortillas and top with the cabbage avocado mixture. Serve topped with fresh cilantro.

Nutrition Info per Serving:
Calories: 230, Protein: 17 g, Fat: 11 g, Carbohydrates: 19 g, Fiber: 4 g, Sugar: 1 g, Sodium: 320 mg

Baked Flounder with Brussels Sprouts

⏱ **PREP TIME:** 10 MINUTES, **COOK TIME:** 10-11 MINUTES, **SERVES:** 2

INGREDIENTS:

- 2 tbsps. olive oil, divided
- 2 (6-ounce, 170g) flounder fillets
- 14 Brussels sprouts
- 1 tbsp. minced fresh garlic
- 3 tbsps. freshly squeezed lemon juice
- ¼ tsp. dried dill
- Salt
- Freshly ground black pepper

DIRECTIONS:

1. Preheat the oven to 400°F(205°C).
2. Rinse the Brussels sprouts and pat them dry. Cut their stem ends off, then cut sprouts in half and place them on a foil-lined baking pan. Drizzle with 1 tbsp. olive oil and toss to coat.
3. Meanwhile, stir together the remaining tbsp. olive oil, lemon juice, garlic and dill in a small bowl.
4. Rinse flounder fillets and pat dry, season lightly with salt and pepper. Place in baking dish and evenly drizzle oil-and-herb mixture over flounder fillets.
5. Bake for 10 to 11 minutes, or until the fish flakes easily when tested with a fork. The Brussels sprouts should be lightly browned and also pierce easily with a fork.
6. Divide the flounder and Brussels sprouts between serving plates.

Nutrition Info per Serving:
Calories: 319, Protein: 29 g, Fat: 17 g, Carbohydrates: 13 g, Fiber: 5 g, Sugar: 2 g, Sodium: 245 mg

---

Cod Chowder with Cauliflower

⏱ **PREP TIME:** 15 MINUTES, **COOK TIME:** 40 MINUTES, **SERVES:** 4

INGREDIENTS:

- 2 tbsps. extra-virgin olive oil
- 1 to 1½ pounds (454g-680g) cod
- 2 pints cherry tomatoes
- 1 medium head cauliflower, coarsely chopped
- 1 leek, white and light green parts only, cut in half lengthwise and sliced thinly
- 2 cups no-salt-added vegetable stock
- ¼ cup green olives, pitted and chopped
- ¼ cup fresh parsley, minced
- 4 garlic cloves, sliced
- 1 tsp. kosher salt
- ¼ tsp. freshly ground black pepper

DIRECTIONS:

1. Heat the olive oil in a Dutch oven or large pot over medium heat. Add the leek and sauté until lightly golden brown for about 5 minutes. Then add the garlic and sauté for 30 seconds. Next add the cauliflower, salt, and black pepper and sauté 2 to 3 minutes.
2. Add the tomatoes and vegetable stock, increase the heat to high and bring to a boil, then turn the heat to low and simmer for 10 minutes.
3. Add the olives and mix together. Add the fish, cover, and simmer 20 minutes, or until fish is opaque and flakes easily.
4. Gently mix in the parsley. Serve hot.

Nutrition Info per Serving:
Calories: 310, Protein: 30 g, Fat: 10 g, Carbohydrates: 22 g, Fiber: 5 g, Sugar: 4 g, Sodium: 445 mg

Shrimp Ceviche with Avocado

PREP TIME: 30 MINUTES, PLUS 30 MINUTES TO MARINATE, **COOK TIME:** 10 MINUTES, **SERVES:** 4

INGREDIENTS:
- 2 pounds (907 g) medium shrimp, peeled, deveined, and cooked
- 2 small roma (plum) tomatoes, seeded and diced
- 1 avocado, pitted, peeled, and chopped
- 1 cup finely chopped red onion
- 1 cup chopped fresh cilantro
- ¾ cup diced cucumber
- ¾ cup fresh lime juice
- ⅓ cup fresh orange juice
- ¼ cup fresh lemon juice

DIRECTIONS:
1. Combine the shrimp, lime juice, lemon juice, and orange juice in a large bowl then cover and refrigerate for 30 minutes.
2. Add the onion, cucumber, tomatoes, cilantro, and avocado to the bowl. Toss to coat and mix evenly.
3. Divide into 4 storage containers.

Nutrition Info per Serving:
Calories: 258, Protein: 40 g, Fat: 6 g, Carbohydrates: 18 g, Fiber: 4 g, Sugar: 4 g, Sodium: 243 mg

Monkfish in Tomato Sauce

PREP TIME: 20 MINUTES, **COOK TIME:** 35 MINUTES, **SERVES:** 4

INGREDIENTS:
- 2 tbsps. extra-virgin olive oil
- 1 to 1½ pounds (454g-680g) monkfish
- 1 (14.5-ounce, 411g) can no-salt-added diced tomatoes
- 3 tbsps. lemon juice, divided
- 1 leek, white and light green parts only, sliced in half lengthwise and thinly sliced
- 2 bulbs fennel, cored and thinly sliced, plus ¼ cup fronds for garnish
- ½ onion, julienned
- 3 garlic cloves, minced
- 2 tbsps. fresh parsley, chopped
- 2 tbsps. fresh oregano, chopped
- ¼ tsp. red pepper flakes
- 1 tsp. kosher salt, divided
- ⅛ tsp. freshly ground black pepper

DIRECTIONS:
1. Place the fish in a medium baking dish and add 2 tbsps. of the lemon juice, ¼ tsp. of the salt, and the black pepper. Place in the refrigerator.
2. Heat the olive oil in a large skillet or sauté pan over medium heat. Add the leek and onion and sauté until translucent, about 3 minutes. Add the garlic and sauté for 30 seconds. Add the fennel and sauté 4 to 5 minutes. Add the tomatoes and simmer for 2 to 3 minutes.
3. Stir in the parsley, oregano, red pepper flakes, the remaining ¾ tsp. salt, and the remaining 1 tbsp. lemon juice. Place the fish on top of the leek mixture, cover and simmer for 20 to 25 minutes, turning over halfway through, until the fish is opaque and pulls apart easily. Garnish with the fennel fronds.

Nutrition Info per Serving:
Calories: 308, Protein: 25 g, Fat: 9 g, Carbohydrates: 14 g, Fiber: 3 g, Sugar: 4 g, Sodium: 345 mg

CHAPTER 4: VEGETABLES

Zoodles with Mediterranean Sauce

PREP TIME: 10 MINUTES, **COOK TIME:** 5 MINUTES, **SERVES:** 2

INGREDIENTS:
- 1 tbsp. olive oil
- 2 zucchinis, spiralized and cooked
- 2 tomatoes, chopped
- ½ avocado, pitted and sliced
- ½ cup roughly chopped fresh parsley
- ½ cup water
- 3 tbsps. ground almonds
- 1 tbsp. fresh rosemary, chopped
- 1 tbsp. apple cider vinegar
- 1 tsp. garlic, smashed
- Salt and ground black pepper, to taste

DIRECTIONS:
1. Add the olive oil, tomatoes, water, parsley, ground almonds, rosemary, apple cider vinegar and garlic to the Instant Pot.
2. Lock the lid. Select the Manual mode and set the cooking time for 5 minutes on High Pressure. When the timer beeps, perform a natural pressure release for 10 minutes, then release any remaining pressure. Carefully open the lid.
3. Divide the cooked zucchini spirals between two serving plates. Spoon the sauce over each serving. Top with the avocado slices and season with salt and black pepper.
4. Serve immediately.

Nutrition Info per Serving:
Calories: 267, Protein: 6 g, Fat: 18 g, Carbohydrates: 20 g, Fiber: 8 g, Sugar: 4 g, Sodium: 19 mg

---

Spiced Eggplant

PREP TIME: 15 MINUTES, **COOK TIME:** 15 MINUTES, **SERVES:** 2

INGREDIENTS:
- Olive oil cooking spray
- 1 large eggplant, cubed
- ½ tsp. dried oregano, crushed
- ½ tsp. dried thyme, crushed
- ½ tsp. dried marjoram, crushed
- ½ tsp. garlic powder
- Salt and black pepper, to taste

DIRECTIONS:
1. Preheat the Air fryer to 390ºF (199ºC) and grease an Air fryer basket.
2. Mix herbs, garlic powder, salt, and black pepper in a bowl.
3. Spray the eggplant cubes with cooking spray and rub with the herb mixture.
4. Arrange the eggplant cubes in the Air fryer basket and air fry for about 15 minutes, flipping twice in between.
5. Dish out onto serving plates and serve hot.

Nutrition Info per Serving:
Calories: 60, Protein: 2 g, Fat: 1 g, Carbohydrates: 13 g, Fiber: 5 g, Sugar: 5 g, Sodium: 183 mg

Roasted Asparagus with Almonds

🕐 **PREP TIME:** 15 MINUTES, **COOK TIME:** 6 MINUTES, **SERVES:** 3

🍷 **INGREDIENTS:**
- 2 tbsps. olive oil
- 1 pound asparagus
- ⅓ cup almonds, sliced
- 2 tbsps. balsamic vinegar
- Salt and black pepper, to taste

👨‍🍳 **DIRECTIONS:**
1. Preheat the Air fryer to 400ºF (204ºC) and grease an Air fryer basket.
2. Mix asparagus, oil, vinegar, salt, and black pepper in a bowl and toss to coat well.
3. Arrange asparagus into the Air fryer basket and sprinkle with the almond slices.
4. Roast for about 6 minutes and dish out to serve hot.

Nutrition Info per Serving:
Calories: 200, Protein: 5 g, Fat: 15 g, Carbohydrates: 14 g, Fiber: 6 g, Sugar: 2 g, Sodium: 150 mg

Stir Fried Zucchini and Bell Pepper

🕐 **PREP TIME:** 10 MINUTES, **COOK TIME:** 7 MINUTES, **SERVES:** 6

🍷 **INGREDIENTS:**
- 1 tbsp. coconut oil
- 2 large zucchinis, sliced
- 2 red sweet bell peppers, julienned
- 1 onion, chopped
- 4 garlic cloves, minced
- Salt and pepper, to taste
- ¼ cup water

👨‍🍳 **DIRECTIONS:**
1. Press the Sauté button on the Instant Pot.
2. Heat the coconut oil and sauté the onion and garlic for 2 minutes or until fragrant.
3. Add the zucchini and red bell peppers.
4. Sprinkle salt and pepper for seasoning.
5. Pour in the water.
6. Lock the lid. Set the Instant Pot to Manual mode, then set the timer for 5 minutes at High Pressure.
7. Once cooking is complete, do a quick pressure release. Carefully open the lid.
8. Serve warm.

Nutrition Info per Serving:
Calories: 27, Protein: 1 g, Fat: 2 g, Carbohydrates: 6 g, Fiber: 1 g, Sugar: 2 g, Sodium: 1 mg

Creamy Spinach with Mushrooms

PREP TIME: 10 MINUTES, **COOK TIME:** 10 MINUTES, **SERVES:** 4

INGREDIENTS:
- 1 tbsp. olive oil
- 10 cups fresh spinach
- 2 cups sliced portabella mushrooms
- 1 cup sliced fennel
- 1 cup unsweetened coconut milk
- ½ cup low-sodium vegetable broth
- 2 cloves garlic, crushed and minced
- ¼ cup white wine
- ½ tsp. salt
- 1 tsp. coarse ground black pepper
- 1 tsp. nutmeg
- ½ tsp. thyme

DIRECTIONS:
1. Press the Sauté button on the Instant Pot and heat the oil. Add the fennel and garlic. Sauté the mixture for 3 minutes.
2. Add the white wine and sauté an additional 2 minutes, or until the wine reduces. Add the remaining ingredients and stir.
3. Lock the lid. Select the Manual mode and set the cooking time for 5 minutes on High Pressure. Once the timer goes off, perform a natural pressure release for 10 minutes, then release any remaining pressure. Carefully open the lid.
4. Stir before serving.

Nutrition Info per Serving:
Calories: 132, Protein: 3 g, Fat: 7 g, Carbohydrates: 15 g, Fiber: 6 g, Sugar: 2 g, Sodium: 192 mg

---

Sweet and Spicy Cauliflower

PREP TIME: 15 MINUTES, **COOK TIME:** 25 MINUTES, **SERVES:** 4

INGREDIENTS:
- 1 head cauliflower, cut into florets
- ¾ cup onion, thinly sliced
- 5 garlic cloves, finely sliced
- 2 scallions, chopped
- 1½ tbsps. soy sauce
- 1 tbsp. rice vinegar
- 1 tbsp. hot sauce
- 1 tsp. coconut sugar
- Pinch of red pepper flakes
- Ground black pepper, as required

DIRECTIONS:
1. Preheat the Air fryer to 350ºF (177ºC) and grease an Air fryer basket.
2. Arrange the cauliflower florets into the Air fryer basket and roast for about 10 minutes.
3. Add the onions and garlic and roast for 10 more minutes.
4. Meanwhile, mix soy sauce, hot sauce, vinegar, coconut sugar, red pepper flakes, and black pepper in a bowl.
5. Pour the soy sauce mixture into the cauliflower mixture.
6. Air fry for about 5 minutes and dish out onto serving plates.
7. Garnish with scallions and serve warm.

Nutrition Info per Serving:
Calories: 54, Protein: 3 g, Fat: 1 g, Carbohydrates: 11 g, Fiber: 4 g, Sugar: 5 g, Sodium: 272 mg

\Chapter 4: Vegetables

Zucchini Fritters

PREP TIME: 10 MINUTES, **COOK TIME:** 8 MINUTES, **SERVES:** 4

INGREDIENTS:
- 1 tbsp. coconut oil
- 2 large zucchinis, grated
- 1 egg, beaten
- 1 daikon, diced
- 1 tsp. ground flax meal
- 1 tsp. salt

DIRECTIONS:
1. In a mixing bowl, combine all the ingredients, except for the coconut oil. Form the zucchini mixture into fritters.
2. Press the Sauté button on the Instant Pot and melt the coconut oil.
3. Place the zucchini fritters in the hot oil and cook for 4 minutes on each side, or until golden brown.
4. Transfer to a plate and serve.

Nutrition Info per Serving:
Calories: 144, Protein: 3 g, Fat: 7 g, Carbohydrates: 18 g, Fiber: 4 g, Sugar: 3 g, Sodium: 372 mg

Spaghetti Squash Noodles with Tomatoes

PREP TIME: 15 MINUTES, **COOK TIME:** 16 TO 18 MINUTES, **SERVES:** 4

INGREDIENTS:
- 2 tbsps. olive oil
- 1 medium spaghetti squash
- 1 cup water
- 1 (14.5-ounce / 411-g) can sugar-free crushed tomatoes
- 1 cup sliced cherry tomatoes
- ¼ cup capers
- 1 small yellow onion, diced
- 6 garlic cloves, minced
- 2 tsps. crushed red pepper flakes
- 2 tsps. dried oregano
- 1 tsp. kosher salt
- ½ tsp. freshly ground black pepper
- 1 tbsp. caper brine
- ½ cup sliced olives

DIRECTIONS:
1. With a sharp knife, halve the spaghetti squash crosswise. Using a spoon, scoop out the seeds and sticky gunk in the middle of each half.
2. Pour the water into the Instant Pot and place the trivet in the pot with the handles facing up. Arrange the squash halves, cut side facing up, on the trivet.
3. Lock the lid. Select the Manual mode and set the cooking time for 7 minutes on High Pressure. When the timer goes off, use a quick pressure release. Carefully open the lid.
4. Remove the trivet and pour out the water that has collected in the squash cavities. Using the tines of a fork, separate the cooked strands into spaghetti-like pieces and set aside in a bowl.
5. Pour the water out of the pot. Select the Sauté mode and heat the oil.
6. Add the onion to the pot and sauté for 3 minutes. Add the garlic, pepper flakes and oregano to the pot and sauté for 1 minute.
7. Stir in the cherry tomatoes, salt and black pepper and cook for 2 minutes, or until the tomatoes are tender.
8. Pour in the crushed tomatoes, capers, caper brine and olives and bring the mixture to a boil. Continue to cook for 2 to 3 minutes to allow the flavors to meld.
9. Stir in the spaghetti squash noodles and cook for 1 to 2 minutes to warm everything through.
10. Transfer the dish to a serving platter and serve.

Nutrition Info per Serving:
Calories: 189, Protein: 5 g, Fat: 9 g, Carbohydrates: 24 g, Fiber: 7 g, Sugar: 4 g, Sodium: 362 mg

Broccoli Rabe with Cilantro and Red Pepper

PREP TIME: 5 MINUTES, **COOK TIME:** 10 MINUTES, **SERVES:** 4

INGREDIENTS:
- 2 tbsps. olive oil
- 14 oz. (397 g) broccoli, sliced into 1-inch pieces
- 3 tbsps. minced fresh cilantro
- 3 garlic cloves, crushed
- ¼ tsp. red pepper, diced
- Salt and pepper

DIRECTIONS:
1. Add a large bowl halfway with ice and water. Set aside.
2. Add 3 quarts water to a large saucepan and bring to a boil. Stir in broccoli rabe to boiling water and add 2 tsps. salt, cook broccoli rabe until wilted and tender, about 2½ minutes. Drain broccoli rabe off, then transfer it to ice water and let rest until chilled. Drain again and pat dry with paper towels.
3. Heat oil, garlic, cilantro and red pepper in a skillet over medium heat, stirring constantly, until garlic starts to sizzle, about 2 minutes. Increase heat to medium-high, whisk in broccoli rabe, stirring to coat with oil, until cooked through, about 1 minute.
4. Spread salt and pepper to season.

Nutrition Info per Serving:
Calories: 110, Protein: 4 g, Fat: 7 g, Carbohydrates: 10 g, Fiber: 4 g, Sugar: 1 g, Sodium: 122 mg

Spinach with Olives

PREP TIME: 15 MINUTES, **COOK TIME:** 2 TO 3 MINUTES, **SERVES:** 4

INGREDIENTS:
- 2 tbsps. olive oil, divided
- Bunch scallions, chopped
- 3 cloves garlic, smashed
- 2 pounds (907 g) spinach, washed
- 1 cup low-sodium vegetable broth
- 1 tbsp. champagne vinegar
- ½ tsp. dried dill weed
- ¼ tsp. cayenne pepper
- Seasoned salt and ground black pepper, to taste
- ½ cup almonds, soaked overnight and drained
- 2 tbsps. green olives, pitted and halved
- 2 tbsps. water
- 2 tsps. lemon juice
- 1 tsp. onion powder
- 1 tsp. garlic powder

DIRECTIONS:
1. Press the Sauté button on the Instant Pot and heat 1 tbsp. olive oil. Add the garlic and scallions to the pot and sauté for 1 to 2 minutes, or until fragrant.
2. Stir in the spinach, vegetable broth, vinegar, dill, cayenne pepper, salt and black pepper.
3. Lock the lid. Select the Manual mode and set the cooking time for 1 minute on High Pressure. When the timer goes off, perform a quick pressure release. Carefully open the lid.
4. Stir in the remaining ingredients.
5. Transfer to serving plates and serve immediately.

Nutrition Info per Serving:
Calories: 186, Protein: 7 g, Fat: 14 g, Carbohydrates: 13 g, Fiber: 5 g, Sugar: 1 g, Sodium: 172 mg

CHAPTER 5: BEAN AND LEGUMES

Tomato and White Beans with Spinach

PREP TIME: 5 MINUTES, **COOK TIME:** 15 MINUTES, **SERVES:** 2

INGREDIENTS:
- 1 tbsp. extra-virgin olive oil
- 1 (13-ounce / 369-g) can white cannellini beans
- 2 cups baby spinach
- ¾ cup crushed tomatoes
- ½ cup low-sodium chicken stock
- 1 large garlic clove, minced
- ½ tsp. dried basil
- ½ tsp. Himalayan salt
- Freshly ground black pepper (optional)

DIRECTIONS:
1. In a small saucepan, heat the olive oil over medium heat.
2. Add the garlic, tomatoes, basil, and salt, and sauté for 3 minutes.
3. Place the beans, stock, and spinach.
4. Cook for 10 minutes more. The liquid will reduce by half.
5. Season with some freshly ground black pepper, if desired. Serve warm.

Nutrition Info per Serving:
Calories: 190, Protein: 9 g, Fat: 6 g, Carbohydrates: 29 g, Fiber: 8 g, Sugar: 4 g, Sodium: 333 mg

Rosemary White Beans

PREP TIME: 8 MINUTES, **COOK TIME:** 8 HOURS, **SERVES:** 16

INGREDIENTS:
- 1 pound (454 g) great northern beans
- 1 onion, finely chopped
- 4 cups water
- 2 cups low sodium vegetable broth
- 3 cloves garlic, minced
- 1 large sprig fresh rosemary
- ½ tsp. salt
- ⅛ tsp. white pepper

DIRECTIONS:
1. Sort over the beans, remove and discard any extraneous material. Rinse the beans well over cold water and drain.
2. In a 6-quart slow cooker, combine the beans, onion, garlic, rosemary, salt, white pepper, water, and vegetable broth.
3. Cover the slow cooker and cook on low for 6 to 8 hours or until the beans are soft.
4. Remove and discard the rosemary stem. Stir in the mixture gently and serve warm.

Nutrition Info per Serving:
Calories: 180, Protein: 10 g, Fat: 0.5 g, Carbohydrates: 31 g, Fiber: 10 g, Sugar: 1 g, Sodium: 192 mg

Triple Bean Chili

PREP TIME: 20 MINUTES, **COOK TIME:** 60 MINUTES, **SERVES:** 8

INGREDIENTS:
- 1 tsp. extra-virgin olive oil
- 1 (15-ounce / 425-g) can sodium-free black beans, rinsed and drained
- 1 (15-ounce / 425-g) can sodium-free red kidney beans, rinsed and drained
- 1 (15-ounce / 425-g) can sodium-free navy beans, rinsed and drained
- 1 (28-ounce / 794-g) can low-sodium diced tomatoes
- 1 sweet onion, chopped
- 1 red bell pepper, seeded and diced
- 1 green bell pepper, seeded and diced
- 2 tsps. minced garlic
- 2 tbsps. chili powder
- 2 tsps. ground cumin
- 1 tsp. ground coriander
- ¼ tsp. red pepper flakes

DIRECTIONS:
1. Place a large saucepan over medium-high heat and add the oil.
2. Sauté the onion, red and green bell peppers, and garlic until the vegetables have softened, about 5 minutes.
3. Add the tomatoes, black beans, red kidney beans, navy beans, chili powder, cumin, coriander, and red pepper flakes to the pan.
4. Bring the chili to a boil, then reduce the heat to low.
5. Simmer the chili, stirring occasionally, for at least 1 hour.
6. Serve hot.

Nutrition Info per Serving:
Calories: 184, Protein: 9 g, Fat: 3 g, Carbohydrates: 34 g, Fiber: 10 g, Sugar: 3 g, Sodium: 216 mg

Red Kidney Beans with Green Beans

PREP TIME: 10 MINUTES, **COOK TIME:** 8 TO 12 MINUTES, **SERVES:** 8

INGREDIENTS:
- 2 tbsps. olive oil
- 1 medium yellow onion, chopped
- 2 cups low-sodium canned red kidney beans, rinsed
- 1 cup roughly chopped green beans
- 1 cup crushed tomatoes
- 2 garlic cloves, minced
- ¼ cup low-sodium vegetable broth
- 1 tsp. smoked paprika
- Salt, to taste

DIRECTIONS:
1. Heat the olive oil in a nonstick skillet over medium heat until shimmering.
2. Add the onion, tomatoes, and garlic. Sauté for 3 to 5 minutes or until fragrant and the onion is translucent.
3. Add the kidney beans, green beans, and broth to the skillet. Sprinkle with paprika and salt, then sauté to combine well.
4. Cover the skillet and cook for 5 to 7 minutes or until the vegetables are tender. Serve immediately.

Nutrition Info per Serving:
Calories: 135, Protein: 7 g, Fat: 6 g, Carbohydrates: 18 g, Fiber: 5 g, Sugar: 3 g, Sodium: 100 mg

Herbs Kidney Bean Stew

⏱ **PREP TIME:** 15 MINUTES, **COOK TIME:** 15 MINUTES, **SERVES:** 2

INGREDIENTS:
- 1 lb. cooked kidney beans
- 1 cup tomato passata
- 3 tbsps. Italian herbs
- 1 cup low-sodium beef broth

DIRECTIONS:
1. Mix all the ingredients in the Instant Pot.
2. Lock the lid. Select the Bean/Chili mode, then set the timer for 15 minutes at High Pressure.
3. Once the timer goes off, do a natural pressure release for 10 minutes, then release any remaining pressure. Carefully open the lid.
4. Serve warm.

Nutrition Info per Serving:
Calories: 250, Protein: 15 g, Fat: 1 g, Carbohydrates: 50 g, Fiber: 16 g, Sugar: 6 g, Sodium: 401 mg

Black-Eyed Peas and Carrot Curry

⏱ **PREP TIME:** 15 MINUTES, **COOK TIME:** 25 MINUTES, **SERVES:** 12

INGREDIENTS:
- 1 tbsp. extra-virgin olive oil
- 1 pound (454 g) dried black-eyed peas, rinsed and drained
- 4 large carrots, coarsely chopped
- 4 cups low-sodium vegetable broth
- 1 cup coconut water
- 1 cup chopped onion
- 1½ tbsps. curry powder
- 1 tbsp. minced garlic
- 1 tsp. peeled and minced fresh ginger
- Kosher salt (optional)
- Lime wedges, for serving

DIRECTIONS:
1. In the electric pressure cooker, combine the black-eyed peas, broth, coconut water, onion, carrots, curry powder, garlic, and ginger. Drizzle the olive oil over the top.
2. Close and lock the lid of the pressure cooker. Set the valve to sealing.
3. Cook on high pressure for 25 minutes.
4. When the cooking is complete, hit Cancel and allow the pressure to release naturally for 10 minutes, then quick release any remaining pressure.
5. Once the pin drops, unlock and remove the lid.
6. Season with salt (if using) and squeeze some fresh lime juice on each serving.

Nutrition Info per Serving:
Calories: 135, Protein: 6 g, Fat: 2 g, Carbohydrates: 25 g, Fiber: 8 g, Sugar: 3 g, Sodium: 290 mg

Chapter 5: Bean and Legumes / 27

Pearl Barley and Black Beans Stew

PREP TIME: 10 MINUTES, **COOK TIME:** 8 HOURS, **SERVES:** 6

INGREDIENTS:

- 2 cups dried black beans, soaked overnight and rinsed
- 1 cup uncooked pearl barley
- 1 avocado, peeled, seeded, and cubed
- 1 onion, chopped
- 1 (14-ounce, 397 g) can diced tomatoes and green chiles, drained
- 4 cups (960 ml) low-sodium vegetable broth
- 1 tsp. garlic powder
- 1 tsp. ground cumin
- 1 tsp. chili powder
- ½ tsp. sea salt

DIRECTIONS:

1. Mix the barley, black beans, broth, garlic powder, cumin, chili powder, onion, tomatoes, and salt in your slow cooker.
2. Cover and cook on low for 8 hours.
3. Garnish with the cubed avocado.

Nutrition Info per Serving:
Calories: 280, Protein: 12 g, Fat: 5 g, Carbohydrates: 43 g, Fiber: 15 g, Sugar: 3 g, Sodium: 290 mg

Roasted Eggplant and Cannellini Beans

PREP TIME: 10 MINUTES, **COOK TIME:** 1 HOUR 10 MINUTES, **SERVES:** 4

INGREDIENTS:

- 1 (16-ounce / 454-g) can cannellini beans, drained and rinsed
- 2 small eggplants, cut into ¼-inch slices
- 3 cups water
- 1 cup hulled barley
- 1 cup arugula
- Juice of 1½ lemons
- 2 garlic cloves, minced
- 3 tbsps. tahini, divided
- 2 tbsps. plus 2 tsps. extra-virgin olive oil, divided
- 3 tsps. tamari, divided
- Sea salt
- Freshly ground black pepper

DIRECTIONS:

1. Preheat the oven to 425°F (220°C).
2. In a large pot, bring the hulled barley, water, and 2 tsps. tamari to a boil over high heat. Once the barley just starts to boil, turn the heat to low and cover the pot.
3. Cook the barley for about 40 minutes without removing the lid. Take the pot from the heat when most of the water has been absorbed and the barley is tender and chewy. Drain well.
4. Pour the remaining tsp. of tamari, 1 tbsp. of tahini, and the lemon juice to the barley. Fluff with a fork, mixing all ingredients, and keep aside.
5. When the barley is cooking, arrange the eggplant slices in a single layer on a parchment paper–lined baking sheet and drizzle with 2 tbsps. olive oil. Season with the salt and pepper before putting into the oven. Bake the slices for about 20 minutes.
6. Add the arugula, the remaining 2 tsps. olive oil, garlic, and remaining 2 tbsps. tahini in a medium skillet over medium heat. Cook for about 5 minutes.
7. Place the cannellini beans to the arugula mixture, and cook for about 5 minutes, until the beans are warm.
8. Put the barley, eggplant, and the arugula-bean mixture into three sections of each bowl, or mix all three components of this bowl together. Enjoy!

Nutrition Info per Serving:
Calories: 390, Protein: 14 g, Fat: 14 g, Carbohydrates: 44 g, Fiber: 15 g, Sugar: 4 g, Sodium: 470 mg

28 \ Chapter 5: Bean and Legumes

Green Lentil and Carrot Stew

PREP TIME: 5 MINUTES, **COOK TIME:** 30 MINUTES, **SERVES:** 4

INGREDIENTS:
- 2 tbsps. extra-virgin olive oil
- 2 cups green lentils, rinsed
- 6 cups water
- 1 yellow onion, chopped
- 1 carrot, chopped
- 2 celery stalks, chopped
- 1 tsp. Himalayan salt
- 1 tbsp. cumin (optional)
- Freshly ground black pepper (optional)

DIRECTIONS:
1. In a sauté pan or skillet, heat the oil over medium heat. Place the carrots, celery, and onion. Cook until the onion is translucent.
2. Place the lentils, salt, cumin (if using), and water. Stir, cover, reduce the heat to low, and sauté for about 25 to 30 minutes.
3. Season with more salt and black pepper, if desired. Serve right away.

Nutrition Info per Serving:
Calories: 210, Protein: 13 g, Fat: 6 g, Carbohydrates: 32 g, Fiber: 15 g, Sugar: 3 g, Sodium: 264 mg

Herbed Black Beans

PREP TIME: 11 MINUTES, **COOK TIME:** 9 HOURS, **SERVES:** 8

INGREDIENTS:
- 3 cups dried black beans, rinsed and drained
- 2 onions, chopped
- 6 cups low-sodium vegetable broth
- 8 garlic cloves, minced
- 1 tsp. dried basil leaves
- ½ tsp. dried thyme leaves
- ½ tsp. dried oregano leaves
- ½ tsp. salt

DIRECTIONS:
1. Mix all the ingredients in a 6-quart slow cooker. Cover the slow cooker and cook on low for 7 to 9 hours, or until the beans have absorbed the liquid and are tender.
2. Remove the bay leaf and discard.

Nutrition Info per Serving:
Calories: 165, Protein: 9 g, Fat: 1 g, Carbohydrates: 29 g, Fiber: 9 g, Sugar: 2 g, Sodium: 183 mg

Chapter 5: Bean and Legumes / 29

CHAPTER 6: EGG DISHES

Asparagus Frittata with Goat Cheese

⏱ **PREP TIME:** *10 MINUTES,* **COOK TIME:** *17 MINUTES,* **SERVES:** *2*

INGREDIENTS:
- 6 large egg whites
- ½ cup asparagus, chopped
- ¼ cup cherry tomatoes, halved
- 2 tbsps. low-fat goat cheese, crumbled
- 1 tbsp. olive oil
- Salt and pepper, to taste

DIRECTIONS:
1. Preheat the oven to 350°F (175°C).
2. Heat olive oil in an oven-safe skillet over medium heat. Add the asparagus and sauté for 4-5 minutes until tender.
3. In a bowl, whisk the egg whites with salt and pepper. Pour the egg whites over the asparagus.
4. Add the cherry tomatoes and sprinkle the goat cheese on top.
5. Transfer the skillet to the oven and bake for 10-12 minutes, until the frittata is set.
6. Serve warm.

Nutrition Info per Serving:
Calories: 138, Protein: 12 g, Fat: 9 g, Carbohydrates: 6 g, Fiber: 2 g, Sugar: 2 g, Sodium: 249 mg

....

Classic Shakshuka

⏱ **PREP TIME:** *10 MINUTES,* **COOK TIME:** *15 MINUTES,* **SERVES:** *2*

INGREDIENTS:
- 4 large eggs
- 1 cup canned diced tomatoes (no added sugar)
- ¼ cup onion, chopped
- ¼ cup bell peppers, diced
- 1 clove garlic, minced
- 1 tsp. paprika
- ½ tsp. cumin
- 1 tbsp. olive oil
- Fresh parsley for garnish

DIRECTIONS:
1. Heat olive oil in a skillet over medium heat. Sauté the onions, garlic, and bell peppers until softened (about 5 minutes).
2. Stir in the diced tomatoes, paprika, and cumin. Simmer for 5 minutes, allowing the sauce to thicken.
3. Make four small wells in the sauce, then crack an egg into each well.
4. Cover the skillet and cook for 5-7 minutes, until the egg whites are set but the yolks are still slightly runny.
5. Garnish with fresh parsley and serve immediately.

Nutrition Info per Serving:
Calories: 248, Protein: 14 g, Fat: 17 g, Carbohydrates: 13 g, Fiber: 3 g, Sugar: 4 g, Sodium: 330 mg

Hard-Boiled Eggs with Cayenne Pepper

PREP TIME: 12 MINUTES (INCLUDES STANDING TIME), **COOK TIME:** 1 MINUTE, **SERVES:** 4

INGREDIENTS:
- 4 hard-boiled eggs, cut in half
- ½ tsp. cayenne pepper
- 1 tbsp. minced basil
- 1 tbsp. olive oil

DIRECTIONS:
1. Add the olive oil in a small, microwave-safe dipping bowl and heat in the microwave in 30-second intervals until hot. Whisk in the cayenne pepper and let sit for 10 minutes.
2. Arrange the egg slices on a platter, spritz with the oil, and top with the basil. Serve immediately.

Nutrition Info per Serving:
Calories: 94, Protein: 6 g, Fat: 8 g, Carbohydrates: 1 g, Fiber: 0 g, Sugar: 0 g, Sodium: 62 mg

Veggie-Packed Scrambled Eggs

PREP TIME: 10 MINUTES, **COOK TIME:** 5 MINUTES, **SERVES:** 2

INGREDIENTS:
- 4 large eggs
- ½ cup spinach, chopped
- ¼ cup bell peppers, diced
- ¼ cup mushrooms, sliced
- 1 tbsp. olive oil
- Salt and pepper, to taste
- 1 tbsp. low-fat cheese (optional)

DIRECTIONS:
1. Whisk the eggs in a bowl with a pinch of salt and pepper.
2. Heat the olive oil in a non-stick pan over medium heat. Sauté the bell peppers and mushrooms until softened (about 3 minutes).
3. Add the spinach and cook until wilted.
4. Pour the eggs into the pan and scramble, stirring continuously, until cooked through (about 2 minutes).
5. Sprinkle with cheese, if using, and serve hot.

Nutrition Info per Serving:
Calories: 217, Protein: 14 g, Fat: 16 g, Carbohydrates: 4 g, Fiber: 1 g, Sugar: 1 g, Sodium: 245 mg

Chapter 6: Egg Dishes / 31

Spinach and Feta Omelet

🕐 **PREP TIME:** 5 MINUTES, **COOK TIME:** 5 MINUTES, **SERVES:** 1

INGREDIENTS:
- 2 large eggs
- ¼ cup fresh spinach, chopped
- 2 tbsps. low-fat feta cheese, crumbled
- 1 tbsp. olive oil
- Salt and pepper, to taste

DIRECTIONS:
1. Beat the eggs with salt and pepper in a bowl.
2. Heat the olive oil in a non-stick skillet over medium heat. Add the spinach and sauté for 1 minute.
3. Pour the eggs into the pan, spreading them evenly.
4. Once the eggs start to set, sprinkle the feta cheese on one half of the omelet.
5. Fold the omelet in half and cook for 1 more minute until fully set.
6. Serve immediately.

Nutrition Info per Serving:
Calories: 267, Protein: 15 g, Fat: 22 g, Carbohydrates: 2 g, Fiber: 0 g, Sugar: 1 g, Sodium: 384 mg

---

Crust Less Broccoli Quiche

🕐 **PREP TIME:** 10 MINUTES, **COOK TIME:** 1 HOUR, **SERVES:** 6

INGREDIENTS:
- 3 large eggs
- 2 cups broccoli florets, chopped
- 1 small onion, diced
- 1 cup low-fat cheddar cheese, grated
- ⅔ cup unsweetened almond milk
- ½ cup low-fat feta cheese, crumbled
- 1 tbsp. extra virgin olive oil
- ½ tsp. sea salt
- ¼ tsp. black pepper
- Nonstick cooking spray

DIRECTIONS:
1. Heat oven to 350ºF (180ºC). Spray a 9-inch baking dish with cooking spray.
2. Heat the oil in a large skillet over medium heat. Add onion and cook for 4 to 5 minutes, until onions are translucent.
3. Add broccoli and stir to combine. Cook until broccoli turns a bright green, about 2 minutes. Transfer to a bowl.
4. In a small bowl, whisk together almond milk, egg, salt, and pepper. Pour over the broccoli. Add the cheddar cheese and stir the together. Pour into the prepared baking dish.
5. Sprinkle the feta cheese over the top and bake for 45 minutes to 1 hour, or until eggs are set in the middle and top is lightly browned. Serve.

Nutrition Info per Serving:
Calories: 78, Protein: 6 g, Fat: 5 g, Carbohydrates: 4 g, Fiber: 1 g, Sugar: 1 g, Sodium: 366 mg

Poached Eggs with Sautéed Kale and Mushrooms

PREP TIME: 10 MINUTES, **COOK TIME:** 15 MINUTES, **SERVES:** 2

INGREDIENTS:
- 4 large eggs
- 2 cups fresh kale, chopped
- ½ cup mushrooms, sliced
- 1 tbsp. olive oil
- 1 tbsp. apple cider vinegar (for poaching)
- Salt and pepper, to taste

DIRECTIONS:
1. Heat olive oil in a skillet over medium heat. Add mushrooms and sauté until browned (about 5 minutes).
2. Add kale and cook until wilted, about 3-4 minutes. Season with salt and pepper, then remove from heat.
3. Bring a pot of water with the vinegar to a simmer. Crack each egg into a small bowl and gently slide it into the simmering water.
4. Poach the eggs for 3-4 minutes until the whites are set but the yolks are still soft.
5. Plate the sautéed kale and mushrooms, then top with the poached eggs.
6. Season with additional salt and pepper, if desired, and serve hot.

Nutrition Info per Serving:
Calories: 243, Protein: 14 g, Fat: 16 g, Carbohydrates: 11 g, Fiber: 3 g, Sugar: 1 g, Sodium: 130 mg

Avocado and Egg Breakfast Bowl

PREP TIME: 10 MINUTES, **COOK TIME:** 10 MINUTES, **SERVES:** 2

INGREDIENTS:
- 2 large eggs, poached or soft-boiled
- 1 ripe avocado, sliced
- ½ cup cherry tomatoes, halved
- ¼ cup baby spinach
- 1 tbsp. olive oil
- 1 tsp. lemon juice
- Salt and pepper, to taste
- 1 tbsp. chia seeds (optional)

DIRECTIONS:
1. Arrange the spinach, cherry tomatoes, and avocado slices in two bowls.
2. Drizzle with olive oil and lemon juice, then season with salt and pepper.
3. Top each bowl with a poached or soft-boiled egg.
4. Sprinkle with chia seeds for added fiber, if desired, and serve immediately.

Nutrition Info per Serving:
Calories: 294, Protein: 12 g, Fat: 20 g, Carbohydrates: 14 g, Fiber: 7 g, Sugar: 2 g, Sodium: 164 mg

Low-Carb Egg Muffins

⏱ **PREP TIME:** 10 MINUTES, **COOK TIME:** 20 MINUTES, **SERVES:** 6

INGREDIENTS:
- 6 large eggs
- ½ cup baby spinach, chopped
- ¼ cup bell peppers, diced
- ¼ cup low-fat cheddar cheese, shredded
- ¼ cup onions, diced
- ¼ tsp. garlic powder
- Salt and pepper, to taste
- Olive oil spray

DIRECTIONS:
1. Preheat the oven to 350°F (175°C). Grease a muffin tin with olive oil spray.
2. In a large bowl, whisk the eggs, garlic powder, salt, and pepper.
3. Fold in the spinach, bell peppers, onions, and cheddar cheese.
4. Pour the egg mixture evenly into the muffin tin cups.
5. Bake for 20 minutes or until the muffins are set and golden brown.
6. Allow them to cool slightly before serving. These can also be refrigerated for up to 3 days.

Nutrition Info per Serving:
Calories: 90, Protein: 7 g, Fat: 6 g, Carbohydrates: 3 g, Fiber: 1 g, Sugar: 1 g, Sodium: 120 mg

---

Egg and Cucumber Salad Wrap

⏱ **PREP TIME:** 10 MINUTES, **COOK TIME:** 0 MINUTES, **SERVES:** 2

INGREDIENTS:
- 4 large eggs, hard-boiled and chopped
- 1 small cucumber, diced
- 2 tbsps. Greek yogurt (plain, unsweetened)
- 1 tsp. Dijon mustard
- ½ tsp. lemon juice
- Salt and pepper, to taste
- 2 large lettuce leaves

DIRECTIONS:
1. In a bowl, mix the chopped hard-boiled eggs, cucumber, Greek yogurt, mustard, and lemon juice. Season with salt and pepper.
2. Spoon the mixture into the lettuce leaves.
3. Roll up and serve immediately.

Nutrition Info per Serving:
Calories: 161, Protein: 14 g, Fat: 10 g, Carbohydrates: 4 g, Fiber: 0 g, Sugar: 1 g, Sodium: 176 mg

Chapter 6: Egg Dishes

CHAPTER 7: POULTRY

Cheese and Spinach Stuffed Chicken Breasts

PREP TIME: 15 MINUTES, **COOK TIME:** 30 MINUTES, **SERVES:** 2

INGREDIENTS:
- 1 tbsp. olive oil
- 2 (4-ounces) skinless, boneless chicken breasts
- 1¾ ounces fresh spinach
- ¼ cup low-fat ricotta cheese, shredded
- 2 tbsps. low-fat cheddar cheese, grated
- Salt and ground black pepper, as required
- ¼ tsp. paprika

DIRECTIONS:
1. Preheat the Air fryer to 390ºF (199ºC) and grease an Air fryer basket.
2. Heat olive oil in a medium skillet over medium heat and cook spinach for about 4 minutes.
3. Add the ricotta and cook for about 1 minute.
4. Cut the slits in each chicken breast horizontally and stuff with the spinach mixture.
5. Season each chicken breast evenly with salt and black pepper and top with cheddar cheese and paprika.
6. Arrange chicken breasts into the Air fryer basket in a single layer and air fry for about 25 minutes.
7. Dish out and serve hot.

Nutrition Info per Serving:
Calories: 325, Protein: 34 g, Fat: 16 g, Carbohydrates: 6 g, Fiber: 1 g, Sugar: 1 g, Sodium: 300 mg

Fried Eggplant with Chicken

PREP TIME: 6 MINUTES, **COOK TIME:** 10 MINUTES, **SERVES:** 6

INGREDIENTS:
- 1 tbsp. coconut oil
- 1 lb. ground chicken
- 3 eggplants, sliced
- 1 tsp. red pepper flakes
- Salt and pepper, to taste

DIRECTIONS:
1. Press the Sauté button on the Instant Pot and heat the coconut oil.
2. Stir in the ground chicken and cook for 3 minutes until lightly golden.
3. Add the remaining ingredients and stir to combine.
4. Lock the lid. Select the Poultry mode and set the cooking time for 6 minutes at High Pressure.
5. Once cooking is complete, do a quick pressure release. Carefully open the lid.
6. Transfer to a large plate and serve warm.

Nutrition Info per Serving:
Calories: 233, Protein: 26 g, Fat: 14 g, Carbohydrates: 14 g, Fiber: 6 g, Sugar: 4 g, Sodium: 278 mg

Thyme Chicken Breasts and Brussels Sprouts

PREP TIME: 10 MINUTES, **COOK TIME:** 25 MINUTES, **SERVES:** 4

INGREDIENTS:
- 1 tbsp. olive oil
- 2 chicken breasts, skinless, boneless and halved
- 2 cups Brussels sprouts, halved
- 1 cup low-sodium chicken stock
- 2 thyme springs, chopped
- A pinch of salt and black pepper

DIRECTIONS:
1. Set your Instant Pot to Sauté and heat the olive oil. Add the chicken breasts and brown for 5 minutes.
2. Add the remaining ingredients to the pot and whisk to combine.
3. Lock the lid. Select the Poultry mode and set the cooking time for 20 minutes at High Pressure.
4. Once cooking is complete, do a natural pressure release for 10 minutes, then release any remaining pressure. Carefully open the lid.
5. Divide the chicken and Brussels sprouts among four plates and serve.

Nutrition Info per Serving:
Calories: 290, Protein: 38 g, Fat: 10 g, Carbohydrates: 10 g, Fiber: 4 g, Sugar: 2 g, Sodium: 339 mg

---

Spicy Chicken and Tomatoes

PREP TIME: 10 MINUTES, **COOK TIME:** 20 MINUTES, **SERVES:** 4

INGREDIENTS:
- 1 tbsp. avocado oil
- 1½ lbs. chicken breast, skinless, boneless, and cubed
- 1 cup tomatoes, cubed
- 1 cup low-sodium chicken stock
- 1 tbsp. smoked paprika
- 1 tsp. cayenne pepper
- A pinch of salt and black pepper

DIRECTIONS:
1. Set your Instant Pot to Sauté and heat the oil. Cook the cubed chicken in the hot oil for 2 to 3 minutes until lightly browned.
2. Add the remaining ingredients to the pot and stir well.
3. Lock the lid. Select the Poultry mode and set the cooking time for 18 minutes at High Pressure.
4. Once cooking is complete, do a natural pressure release for 10 minutes, then release any remaining pressure. Carefully open the lid.
5. Serve the chicken and tomatoes in bowls while warm.

Nutrition Info per Serving:
Calories: 358, Protein: 52 g, Fat: 12 g, Carbohydrates: 11 g, Fiber: 2 g, Sugar: 3 g, Sodium: 337 mg

Chicken and Veggie Kabobs

PREP TIME: 20 MINUTES, PLUS 3 HOURS MARINATING TIME, **COOK TIME:** 30 MINUTES, **SERVES:** 3

INGREDIENTS:
- 1 tbsp. olive oil
- 1 lb. skinless, boneless chicken thighs, cut into cubes
- 2 small tomatoes, seeded and cut into large chunks
- 1 large red onion, cut into large chunks
- ½ cup plain Greek yogurt
- Wooden skewers, presoaked
- 2 tsps. curry powder
- ½ tsp. smoked paprika
- ¼ tsp. cayenne pepper
- Salt, to taste

DIRECTIONS:
1. Preheat the Air fryer to 360°F (182°C) and grease an Air fryer basket.
2. Mix the chicken, oil, yogurt, and spices in a large baking dish.
3. Thread chicken cubes, tomatoes and onion onto presoaked wooden skewers.
4. Coat the skewers generously with marinade and refrigerate for about 3 hours.
5. Transfer half of the skewers in the Air fryer basket and roast for about 15 minutes.
6. Repeat with the remaining skewers.
7. Dish out to serve warm.

Nutrition Info per Serving:
Calories: 383, Protein: 30 g, Fat: 21 g, Carbohydrates: 12 g, Fiber: 2 g, Sugar: 5 g, Sodium: 360 mg

Jamaican Curry Chicken Drumsticks

PREP TIME: 5 MINUTES, **COOK TIME:** 20 MINUTES, **SERVES:** 4

INGREDIENTS:
- 1½ pounds (680 g) chicken drumsticks
- 1 cup low-sodium chicken stock
- ½ medium onion, diced
- 1 tbsp. Jamaican curry powder
- 1 tsp. salt
- ½ tsp. dried thyme

DIRECTIONS:
1. Sprinkle the salt and curry powder over the chicken drumsticks.
2. Place the chicken drumsticks into the Instant Pot, along with the remaining ingredients.
3. Secure the lid. Select the Manual mode and set the cooking time for 20 minutes at High Pressure.
4. Once cooking is complete, do a quick pressure release. Carefully open the lid. Serve warm.

Nutrition Info per Serving:
Calories: 367, Protein: 42 g, Fat: 19 g, Carbohydrates: 5 g, Fiber: 1 g, Sugar: 1 g, Sodium: 498 mg

Chapter 7: Poultry / 37

Spiced Roasted Whole Chicken

PREP TIME: 15 MINUTES, **COOK TIME:** 1 HOUR, **SERVES:** 6

INGREDIENTS:
- 3 tbsps. olive oil
- 1 (5-pounds) whole chicken, necks and giblets removed
- 2 tsps. dried thyme
- 2 tsps. paprika
- 1 tsp. onion powder
- 1 tsp. garlic powder
- 1 tsp. cayenne pepper
- 1 tsp. ground white pepper
- Salt and ground black pepper, as required

DIRECTIONS:
1. Preheat the Air fryer to 350ºF (177ºC) and grease an Air fryer basket.
2. Mix the thyme, spices and other seasoning in a bowl.
3. Coat the chicken generously with olive oil and rub with spice mixture.
4. Arrange the chicken into the Air Fryer basket, breast side down and roast for about 30 minutes.
5. Flip the chicken and roast for 30 more minutes.
6. Dish out the chicken in a platter and cut into desired size pieces to serve.

Nutrition Info per Serving:
Calories: 450, Protein: 42 g, Fat: 30 g, Carbohydrates: 1 g, Fiber: 0 g, Sugar: 0 g, Sodium: 200 mg

Creamy Chicken with Mushrooms

PREP TIME: 12 MINUTES, **COOK TIME:** 11 MINUTES, **SERVES:** 6

INGREDIENTS:
- 4 garlic cloves, minced
- 6 boneless chicken breasts, halved
- ½ cup unsweetened coconut milk
- 1 cup mushrooms, sliced
- 1 onion, chopped
- ½ cup water
- Salt and pepper to taste

DIRECTIONS:
1. Press the Sauté button on the Instant Pot and stir in the chicken breasts.
2. Fold in the onions and garlic and sauté for at least 3 minutes until tender. Season with salt and pepper. Add the remaining ingredients to the Instant Pot and whisk well.
3. Lock the lid. Select the Poultry mode and cook for 8 minutes at High Pressure.
4. Once cooking is complete, do a natural pressure release for 5 minutes, then release any remaining pressure. Carefully open the lid.
5. Allow to cool for 5 minutes before serving.

Nutrition Info per Serving:
Calories: 270, Protein: 36 g, Fat: 10 g, Carbohydrates: 6 g, Fiber: 1 g, Sugar: 1 g, Sodium: 120 mg

Buffalo Chicken Wings

PREP TIME: 20 MINUTES, **COOK TIME:** 22 MINUTES, **SERVES:** 6

INGREDIENTS:
- 1 tbsp. olive oil
- 2 pounds chicken wings, cut into drumettes and flats
- ¼ cup red hot sauce
- 2 tbsps. low-sodium soy sauce
- 1 tsp. chicken seasoning
- 1 tsp. garlic powder
- Ground black pepper, to taste

DIRECTIONS:
1. Preheat the Air fryer to 400ºF (204ºC) and grease an Air fryer basket.
2. Season each chicken wing evenly with chicken seasoning, garlic powder, and black pepper.
3. Arrange the chicken wings into the Air Fryer basket and drizzle with olive oil.
4. Roast for about 10 minutes and dish out the chicken wings onto a serving platter.
5. Pour the red hot sauce and soy sauce on the chicken wings and toss to coat well.
6. Roast for about 12 minutes and dish out to serve hot.

Nutrition Info per Serving:
Calories: 410, Protein: 32 g, Fat: 30 g, Carbohydrates: 6 g, Fiber: 0 g, Sugar: 0 g, Sodium: 491 mg

Crispy Herbed Turkey Breast

PREP TIME: 5 MINUTES, **COOK TIME:** 30 MINUTES, **SERVES:** 2

INGREDIENTS:
- 2 turkey breasts
- ½ tbsp. fresh rosemary, chopped
- ½ tbsp. fresh parsley, chopped
- 1 garlic clove, minced
- 1 tbsp. ginger, minced
- 1 tsp. five spice powder
- Salt and black pepper, to taste

DIRECTIONS:
1. Preheat the Air fryer to 340ºF (171ºC) and grease an Air fryer basket.
2. Mix garlic, herbs, five spice powder, salt and black pepper in a bowl.
3. Brush the turkey breasts generously with garlic mixture and transfer into the Air fryer.
4. Air fry for about 25 minutes and set the Air fryer to 390ºF (199ºC).
5. Air fry for about 5 more minutes and dish out to serve warm.

Nutrition Info per Serving:
Calories: 300, Protein: 62 g, Fat: 4 g, Carbohydrates: 2 g, Fiber: 0 g, Sugar: 0 g, Sodium: 247 mg

Chapter 7: Poultry / 39

CHAPTER 8: LEAN MEATS AND TOFU

Garlicky Tofu and Brussels Sprouts

PREP TIME: 20 MINUTES, **COOK TIME:** 30 MINUTES, **SERVES:** 4

INGREDIENTS:
- Nonstick cooking spray
- 1 (14-ounce / 397-g) package extra-firm organic tofu, drained and cut into 1-inch pieces
- 1 pound (454 g) Brussels sprouts, quartered
- ½ cup dried cherries
- ¼ cup roasted salted pumpkin seeds
- 2 tbsps. balsamic vinegar
- 1 tbsp. extra-virgin olive oil
- 1 tbsp. garlic, minced
- 1 tbsp. balsamic glaze
- ¼ tsp. salt
- ¼ tsp. black pepper, freshly ground

DIRECTIONS:
1. Preheat the oven to 400ºF (205ºC). Line a large baking sheet with foil and coat it with cooking spray.
2. Place the tofu pieces between 2 clean towels. Rest for 15 minutes to wick away additional liquid.
3. In a large bowl, whisk the vinegar, oil, garlic, salt, and pepper. Add the tofu and Brussels sprouts and toss gently. Transfer the ingredients to the baking sheet and evenly spread into a layer. Roast for 20 minutes.
4. Remove from the oven and toss its contents. Sprinkle the cherries and pumpkin seeds on top of the Brussels sprouts and tofu. Return to the oven and roast for an additional 10 minutes. Remove from the oven and drizzle with balsamic glaze. Toss to coat.
5. Serve immediately.

Nutrition Info per Serving:
Calories: 296, Protein: 15 g, Fat: 20 g, Carbohydrates: 33 g, Fiber: 7 g, Sugar: 10 g, Sodium: 197 mg

---

Beef and Cauliflower

PREP TIME: 12 MINUTES, **COOK TIME:** 35 MINUTES, **SERVES:** 4

INGREDIENTS:
- 1 tbsp. extra virgin olive oil
- 1½ lbs. ground beef
- 6 cups cauliflower, cut into florets
- 1 cup puréed tomato
- 1 cup water
- 1 tsp. salt

DIRECTIONS:
1. Set the Instant Pot to Sauté setting, then add the olive oil and heat until shimmering.
2. Add the beef and sauté for 4 or 5 minutes or until browned.
3. Add the rest of the ingredients.
4. Lock the lid. Select the Manual setting and set the timer at 30 minutes on High Pressure.
5. When the timer beeps, press Cancel, then use a quick pressure release.
6. Carefully open the lid and allow to cool for a few minutes. Serve warm.

Nutrition Info per Serving:
Calories: 290, Protein: 30 g, Fat: 16 g, Carbohydrates: 10 g, Fiber: 4 g, Sugar: 3 g, Sodium: 482 mg

Tofu and Broccoli Stir-Fry

PREP TIME: 10 MINUTES, **COOK TIME:** 10 MINUTES, **SERVES:** 4

INGREDIENTS:
- 3 tbsps. extra-virgin olive oil
- 12 ounces (340 g) firm tofu, cut into ½-inch pieces
- 4 cups broccoli, broken into florets
- 4 scallions, sliced
- 4 garlic cloves, minced
- ¼ cup low-sodium vegetable broth
- 2 tbsps. soy sauce (use gluten-free soy sauce if necessary)
- 1 tsp. peeled and grated fresh ginger
- 1 cup cooked brown rice

DIRECTIONS:
1. In a large skillet over medium-high heat, heat the olive oil until it shimmers.
2. Add the scallions, tofu, and broccoli and cook, stirring, until the vegetables begin to soften, about 6 minutes. Add the garlic and ginger and cook, stirring constantly, for 30 seconds.
3. Add the broth, soy sauce, and rice. Cook, stirring, 1 to 2 minutes more to heat the rice through.

Nutrition Info per Serving:
Calories: 235, Protein: 12 g, Fat: 14 g, Carbohydrates: 21 g, Fiber: 5 g, Sugar: 2 g, Sodium: 362 mg

Healthy Tempeh Lettuce Wraps

PREP TIME: 5 MINUTES, **COOK TIME:** 5 MINUTES, **SERVES:** 2

INGREDIENTS:
- 1 tbsp. olive oil
- 1 package tempeh, crumbled
- 1 head butter-leaf lettuce
- ½ onion, diced
- ½ red bell pepper, diced
- 1 tbsp. garlic, diced fine
- 1 tbsp. low-sodium soy sauce
- 1 tsp. ginger,
- 1 tsp. onion powder
- 1 tsp. garlic powder

DIRECTIONS:
1. Heat oil and garlic in a large skillet over medium heat.
2. Add onion, tempeh, and bell pepper and sauté for 3 minutes.
3. Add soy sauce and spices and cook for another 2 minutes.
4. Spoon mixture into lettuce leaves.

Nutrition Info per Serving:
Calories: 131, Protein: 8 g, Fat: 5 g, Carbohydrates: 14 g, Fiber: 7 g, Sugar: 4 g, Sodium: 268 mg

Chapter 8: Lean Meats and Tofu

Curried Tofu

PREP TIME: 10 MINUTES, **COOK TIME:** 2 HOURS, **SERVES:** 4

INGREDIENTS:
- 1 cup firm tofu, cut into cubes
- 2 cup green bell pepper, diced
- 1 onion, peeled and diced
- 1 cup tomato paste
- 1½ cups canned unsweetened coconut milk
- 2 cloves garlic, diced fine
- 2 tbsps. raw peanut butter
- 1 tbsp. garam masala
- 1 tbsp. curry powder
- 1½ tsps. salt

DIRECTIONS:
1. Add all the ingredients, except the tofu to a blender or food processor. Process until thoroughly combined.
2. Pour into a crock pot and add the tofu. Cover and cook on high for 2 hours.
3. Stir well and serve over cauliflower rice.

Nutrition Info per Serving:
Calories: 389, Protein: 13 g, Fat: 28 g, Carbohydrates: 28 g, Fiber: 5 g, Sugar: 8 g, Sodium: 416 mg

Pork Tenderloin with Paprika-Mustard

PREP TIME: 10 MINUTES, **COOK TIME:** 20 MINUTES, **SERVES:** 6

INGREDIENTS:
- 2 tbsps. olive oil
- 2 (1 lb. each) pork tenderloins
- 1 tsp. salt
- 1½ tsps. smoked paprika
- 2 tbsps. Dijon mustard

DIRECTIONS:
1. Combine the mustard, oil, salt and paprika in a small bowl.
2. Heat the griddle grill to medium heat.
3. Rub the tenderloins with the mustard mixture and coat evenly.
4. Arrange the tenderloins on the griddle and cook until browned on both sides, about 15-20 minutes, until the internal temperature is 135°F(57°C).
5. Transfer the tenderloins to a plate and let rest for 5 minutes before slicing and serving.

Nutrition Info per Serving:
Calories: 301, Protein: 30 g, Fat: 18 g, Carbohydrates: 2 g, Fiber: 0 g, Sugar: 0 g, Sodium: 426 mg

Chapter 8: Lean Meats and Tofu

Teriyaki Tofu Burger

⏲ **PREP TIME:** 15 MINUTES, **COOK TIME:** 15 MINUTES, **SERVES:** 2

🍷 **INGREDIENTS:**
- 2 (3-ounce / 85-g) tofu portions, extra firm, pressed between paper towels 15 minutes
- ¼ red onion, sliced
- 2 tbsps. carrot, grated
- 1 tbsp. teriyaki marinade
- 1 tbsp. Sriracha
- 1 tsp. red chili flakes
- 1 tsp. almond butter
- Butter leaf lettuce, for serving
- 2 whole wheat sandwich thins

🍳 **DIRECTIONS:**
1. Heat grill to a medium heat.
2. Marinate tofu in teriyaki marinade, red chili flakes and Sriracha.
3. Melt almond butter in a small skillet over medium-high heat. Add onions and cook until caramelized, about 5 minutes.
4. Grill tofu for 3 to 4 minutes per side.
5. To assemble, place tofu on bottom roll. Top with lettuce, carrot, and onion. Add top of the roll and serve.

Nutrition Info per Serving:
Calories: 230, Protein: 12 g, Fat: 11 g, Carbohydrates: 28 g, Fiber: 5 g, Sugar: 3 g, Sodium: 480 mg

Beef Tips with Portobello Mushrooms

⏲ **PREP TIME:** 20 MINUTES, **COOK TIME:** 26 MINUTES, **SERVES:** 4

🍷 **INGREDIENTS:**
- 2 tsps. olive oil
- 1 beef top sirloin steak (1-pound / 454-g), cubed
- ½ pound (227 g) sliced baby portobello mushrooms
- 1 small onion, halved and sliced
- 2 cups low-sodium beef broth
- ⅓ cup dry red wine
- ¼ cup cold water
- 3 to 4 tbsps. cornstarch
- 1 tbsp. Worcestershire sauce
- ½ tsp. salt
- ¼ tsp. ground black pepper

🍳 **DIRECTIONS:**
1. Select the Sauté setting of the Instant Pot. Add the olive oil.
2. Sprinkle the beef with salt and pepper. Brown meat in batches in the pot for 10 minutes. Flip constantly. Transfer meat to a bowl.
3. Add the wine to the pot. Return beef to the pot and add mushrooms, onion, broth, and Worcestershire sauce.
4. Lock the lid. Select the Manual setting and set the cooking time for 15 minutes at High Pressure.
5. When timer beeps, quick release the pressure. Carefully open the lid.
6. Select the Sauté setting and bring to a boil.
7. Meanwhile, in a small bowl, mix cornstarch and water until smooth.
8. Gradually stir the cornstarch into beef mixture. Sauté for 1 more minute or until sauce is thickened. Serve immediately.

Nutrition Info per Serving:
Calories: 312, Protein: 32 g, Fat: 14 g, Carbohydrates: 10 g, Fiber: 1 g, Sugar: 2 g, Sodium: 405 mg

Chapter 8: Lean Meats and Tofu / 43

Grilled Tofu Skewers

🕐 **PREP TIME:** 15 MINUTES, PLUS 15 MINUTES MARINATING TIME, **COOK TIME:** 15 MINUTES, **SERVES:** 6

INGREDIENTS:
- 1 block tofu
- 2 cups cherry tomatoes
- 2 small zucchini, sliced
- 1 red onion, cut into 1-inch cubes
- 1 red bell pepper, cut into 1-inch cubes
- 1 yellow bell pepper, cut into 1-inch cubes
- 2 tbsps. lite soy sauce
- 3 tsps. barbecue sauce
- 2 tsps. sesame seeds
- Salt and ground black pepper, to taste
- Nonstick cooking spray

DIRECTIONS:
1. Press tofu to extract liquid, for about half an hour. Then, cut tofu into cubes and marinate in soy sauce for at least 15 minutes.
2. Heat the grill to medium-high heat. Spray the grill rack with cooking spray.
3. Assemble skewers with tofu alternating with vegetables.
4. Grill for 2 to 3 minutes per side until vegetables start to soften, and tofu is golden brown. At the very end of cooking time, season with salt and pepper and brush with barbecue sauce. Serve garnished with sesame seeds.

Nutrition Info per Serving:
Calories: 160, Protein: 9 g, Fat: 6 g, Carbohydrates: 14 g, Fiber: 4 g, Sugar: 3 g, Sodium: 237 mg

---

Sun-dried Tomato Crusted Chops

🕐 **PREP TIME:** 10 MINUTES, PLUS 1 HOUR MARINATING TIME, **COOK TIME:** 12 MINUTES, **SERVES:** 4

INGREDIENTS:
- ½ cup olive oil, plus more for brushing
- 4 center-cut boneless pork chops (about 1¼ pounds / 567 g)
- ½ cup toasted almonds
- ½ cup oil-packed sun-dried tomatoes
- ¼ cup grated low-fat Parmesan cheese
- 2 tbsps. water
- ½ tsp. salt
- Freshly ground black pepper, to taste

DIRECTIONS:
1. Place the sun-dried tomatoes into a food processor and pulse them until they are coarsely chopped. Put the Parmesan cheese, almonds, olive oil, water, salt and pepper. Process into a smooth paste.
2. Coat most of the paste (leave a little in reserve) onto both sides of the pork chops and then pierce the meat several times with a fork. Let the pork chops marinate for at least 1 hour (refrigerate if marinating for longer than 1 hour).
3. Bring the griddle grill to high heat.
4. Brush more olive oil on the griddle and place the pork chops. Cook for about 6 minutes per side, flipping once during cooking.
5. Remove the pork chops from the griddle and serve warm.

Nutrition Info per Serving:
Calories: 420, Protein: 30 g, Fat: 28 g, Carbohydrates: 10 g, Fiber: 2 g, Sugar: 2 g, Sodium: 389 mg

44 \ Chapter 8: Lean Meats and Tofu

CHAPTER 9: SALADS

Rice Cauliflower Tabbouleh Salad

PREP TIME: 15 MINUTES, **COOK TIME:** 0, **SERVES:** 4

INGREDIENTS:
- ¼ cup extra-virgin olive oil
- 1 pound (454g) riced cauliflower
- 12 cherry tomatoes, halved
- 1 English cucumber, diced
- 1 cup fresh parsley, chopped
- ½ cup fresh mint, chopped
- ¼ cup lemon juice
- Zest of 1 lemon
- ¾ tsp. kosher salt
- ½ tsp. ground turmeric
- ¼ tsp. ground coriander
- ¼ tsp. ground cumin
- ¼ tsp. black pepper
- ⅛ tsp. ground cinnamon

DIRECTIONS:
1. In a large bowl, whisk together the olive oil, lemon juice, lemon zest, salt, turmeric, coriander, cumin, black pepper, and cinnamon.
2. Add the riced cauliflower to the bowl and mix well. Put the cucumber, tomatoes, parsley, and mint and gently mix together.

Nutrition Info per Serving:
Calories: 210, Protein: 3 g, Fat: 18 g, Carbohydrates: 13 g, Fiber: 5 g, Sugar: 2 g, Sodium: 260 mg

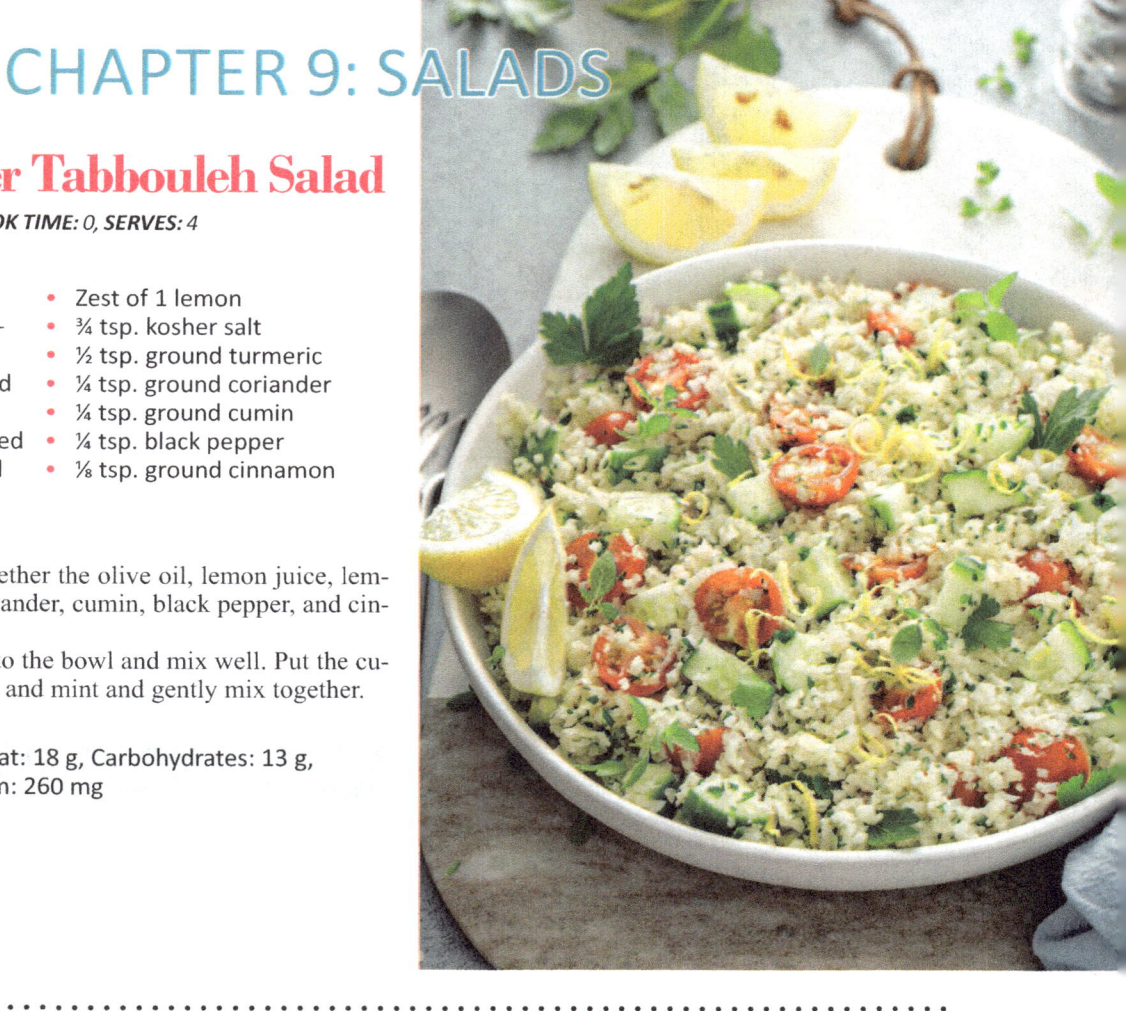

Quick Summer Chicken Salad

PREP TIME: 15 MINUTES, **COOK TIME:** CHILL 1 HOUR, **SERVES:** 6

INGREDIENTS:
- 3 cups cooked, skinless chicken breast
- ½ cup chopped apple
- ½ cup chopped celery
- ¼ cup low-fat mayonnaise
- ¼ cup chopped almonds
- 2 tsps. chopped fresh sage
- 2 tsps. chopped fresh cilantro

DIRECTIONS:
1. Combine all the ingredients in a bowl and stir until combined.
2. Chill for an hour before serving.

Nutrition Info per Serving:
Calories: 290, Protein: 26 g, Fat: 16 g, Carbohydrates: 12 g, Fiber: 2 g, Sugar: 2 g, Sodium: 276 mg

Lemony Kale and Tomato Salad

PREP TIME: 10 MINUTES, **COOK TIME:** 10 MINUTES, **SERVES:** 4

INGREDIENTS:
- 1½ tbsps. olive oil, divided
- 2 heads kale
- 1 cup cherry tomatoes, sliced
- Juice of 1 lemon
- 2 cloves garlic, minced
- Sea salt and freshly ground pepper

DIRECTIONS:
1. Wash and dry kale.
2. Tear the kale into small pieces.
3. Heat 1 tbsp. olive oil in a large skillet, and add the garlic. Cook for 1 minute and then add the kale.
4. Add the tomatoes after kale wilted.
5. Cook until tomatoes are softened, then remove from heat.
6. Put tomatoes and kale together in a bowl, and season with sea salt and freshly ground pepper.
7. Drizzle with remaining olive oil and lemon juice, serve.

Nutrition Info per Serving:
Calories: 120, Protein: 4 g, Fat: 8 g, Carbohydrates: 10 g, Fiber: 3 g, Sugar: 2 g, Sodium: 120 mg

Endive and Shrimp with Walnuts

PREP TIME: 2 HOURS, **COOK TIME:** 10 MINUTES, **SERVES:** 4

INGREDIENTS:
- ¼ cup (60 ml) olive oil
- 1 small shallot, minced
- 1 tbsp. Dijon mustard
- Juice and zest of 1 lemon
- Sea salt and freshly ground pepper
- 2 cups (480 ml) salted water
- 14 shrimp, peeled and deveined
- 1 head endive
- ½ cup tart green apple, diced
- 2 tbsps. toasted walnuts

DIRECTIONS:
1. For the vinaigrette, whisk together the first five ingredients in a small bowl until creamy.
2. Refrigerate for at least 2 hours.
3. Boil salted water in a small pan. Put in the shrimp and cook for 1–2 minutes, or until the shrimp turns pink. Drain and cool down under cold water.
4. Wash and break the endive. Place on plates and top with the shrimp, toasted walnuts and green apple.
5. Drizzle with the vinaigrette before serving.

Nutrition Info per Serving:
Calories: 195, Protein: 10 g, Fat: 16 g, Carbohydrates: 8 g, Fiber: 3 g, Sugar: 2 g, Sodium: 193 mg

Healthy Southwestern Salad

PREP TIME: 15 MINUTES, **COOK TIME:** 20 MINUTES, **SERVES:** 5

INGREDIENTS:
- 2 tbsps. olive oil
- 1 can black beans
- 1 can red beans
- 4 fresh tomatoes, sliced
- 1 cup diced red peppers
- ½ cup chopped fresh cilantro
- 2 tbsps. white wine vinegar
- 1 tsp. hot sauce
- Black pepper and cumin

DIRECTIONS:
1. Open the cans of beans and rinse them thoroughly with cool water. Combine the beans in a serving bowl.
2. Add the tomatoes, cilantro and red pepper to the beans. Sprinkle generously with black pepper and cumin. Whisk together the oil, vinegar and hot sauce in a small bowl and drizzle over the salad. Toss gently, cover and chill.
3. Let the salad stand, covered at room temperature for 20 minutes before serving.

Nutrition Info per Serving:
Calories: 138, Protein: 5 g, Fat: 6 g, Carbohydrates: 16 g, Fiber: 8 g, Sugar: 3 g, Sodium: 239 mg

Shredded Beef Salad

PREP TIME: 10 MINUTES, **COOK TIME:** 8 HOURS, **SERVES:** 6

INGREDIENTS:
- 1 pound (454 g) flank steak
- 2 red bell peppers, seeded and thinly sliced
- 8 cups shredded iceberg lettuce
- 1 cup (240 ml) low-sodium beef broth
- 2 tsps. freshly ground black pepper
- 1 tsp. garlic powder
- 1 tsp. smoked paprika
- ½ tsp. ground coriander
- ½ tsp. sea salt
- ⅛ tsp. cayenne pepper

DIRECTIONS:
1. Mix the black pepper, garlic powder, paprika, coriander, salt, and cayenne in a small bowl.
2. Spread the mixture evenly over the flank steak, rubbing it in.
3. Combine the seasoned flank steak, bell peppers, and broth in the slow cooker.
4. Cover and cook on low for 8 hours.
5. Remove the beef from the sauce and shred it with forks.
6. Put the beef back to the sauce and mix well.
7. Serve the shredded beef on top of the shredded lettuce, with sauce drizzled on top.

Nutrition Info per Serving:
Calories: 290, Protein: 21 g, Fat: 15 g, Carbohydrates: 12 g, Fiber: 3 g, Sugar: 3 g, Sodium: 384 mg

Chapter 9: Salads / 47

Fresh Raspberry Spinach Salad

PREP TIME: 10 MINUTES, **COOK TIME:** 30 MINUTES, **SERVES:** 2

INGREDIENTS:
- 1 (6-ounce, 170g) bag baby spinach
- 1 Asian pear, cut into bite-sized pieces
- 1 cup fresh red raspberries
- ½ cup whole walnuts
- ¼ cup low-fat blue cheese crumbles
- ¼ cup low-fat Italian dressing

DIRECTIONS:
1. Toss all ingredients, let stand at room temperature for 30 minutes before serving.
2. Toss again right before plating.

Nutrition Info per Serving:
Calories: 220, Protein: 6 g, Fat: 15 g, Carbohydrates: 18 g, Fiber: 4 g, Sugar: 6 g, Sodium: 250 mg

---

Thai Chicken Salad

PREP TIME: 10 MINUTES, **COOK TIME:** CHILL 30 MINUTES, **SERVES:** 4

INGREDIENTS:
- ¼ cup olive oil
- ¾ pound (340g) chicken breast, cooked
- 1 small cucumber, chopped
- ¾ cup brown rice, cooked
- ¾ cup fresh lime juice
- ½ cup unsalted, roasted cashews
- ½ cup cilantro, chopped
- 2 green onions, chopped
- ¼ cup fresh mint, chopped
- ¼ cup red onion, diced
- ¼ tsp. cayenne pepper
- 1 head romaine lettuce, chopped

DIRECTIONS:
1. Toss to combine all the ingredients except the cayenne and romaine in a large serving bowl.
2. Sprinkle with cayenne, then toss with the romaine and chill for 30 minutes before serving.

Nutrition Info per Serving:
Calories: 350, Protein: 23 g, Fat: 20 g, Carbohydrates: 21 g, Fiber: 3 g, Sugar: 2 g, Sodium: 200 mg

48 \ Chapter 9: Salads

Healthy Tuna Salad

PREP TIME: 15 MINUTES, **COOK TIME:** 0 MINUTES, **SERVES:** 4

INGREDIENTS:
- 2 (6-ounce (170g)) cans albacore tuna in water, no salt added, drained
- ¼ cup chopped Roma tomato
- ½ jalapeño chile pepper, seeded and chopped
- 1 small avocado, thinly sliced
- ¼ cup chopped red onion
- ¼ cup chopped celery
- 3 tbsps. low-fat plain Greek yogurt
- 1 tsp. brown mustard
- ⅛ tsp. cracked black pepper

DIRECTIONS:
1. In a medium bowl, combine the celery, chile pepper, tomato, and onion. Mix in the tuna, mustard, yogurt, and black pepper until well combined.
2. Top the salad with avocado slices, and serve.

Nutrition Info per Serving:
Calories: 212, Protein: 22 g, Fat: 10 g, Carbohydrates: 8 g, Fiber: 4 g, Sugar: 1 g, Sodium: 151 mg

Grilled Romaine Salad with Walnuts

PREP TIME: 5 MINUTES, **COOK TIME:** 10 MINUTES, **SERVES:** 4

INGREDIENTS:
- 2 tbsps. olive oil
- 1 head romaine lettuce (about 12 leaves)
- ½ cup halved cherry tomatoes
- ¼ cup low-fat feta cheese
- ¼ cup chopped walnuts
- 2 tbsps. balsamic vinaigrette

DIRECTIONS:
1. Separate the leaves from the romaine head, and wash and dry them.
2. Heat a grill to medium-high, brush oil on both sides of each lettuce leaf, and place on the grill. Watch carefully and turn often, as the leaves can wilt quickly.
3. Once char marks are visible, remove the leaves and place three leaves on four individual plates.
4. Top the grilled lettuce with the cheese, tomatoes, and walnuts. Drizzle with 2 tbsps. balsamic vinaigrette, and serve.

Nutrition Info per Serving:
Calories: 160, Protein: 5 g, Fat: 12 g, Carbohydrates: 10 g, Fiber: 3 g, Sugar: 2 g, Sodium: 209 mg

Chapter 9: Salads / 49

CHAPTER 10: SOUP AND STEW

Spicy Butternut Squash Soup

PREP TIME: 15 MINUTES, **COOK TIME:** 8 HOURS, **SERVES:** 6

INGREDIENTS:
- 1 butternut squash, peeled, seeded, and diced
- 1 onion, chopped
- 1 sweet-tart apple (such as Braeburn), peeled, cored, and chopped
- 3 cups (720 ml) low-sodium vegetable broth, or store bought
- ½ cup (120 ml) unsweetened almond milk
- 1 tsp. garlic powder
- ½ tsp. ground sage
- ¼ tsp. sea salt
- ¼ tsp. freshly ground black pepper
- Pinch cayenne pepper
- Pinch nutmeg

DIRECTIONS:
1. In your slow cooker, mix the squash, broth, garlic powder, sage, salt, black pepper, onion, apple, cayenne, and nutmeg.
2. Cover and cook on low for 8 hours.
3. Using an immersion blender or food processor, purée the soup, adding the milk. Stir to combine, and serve.

Nutrition Info per Serving:
Calories: 165, Protein: 3 g, Fat: 4 g, Carbohydrates: 31 g, Fiber: 6 g, Sugar: 6 g, Sodium: 302 mg

---

Chicken and Zoodles Soup

PREP TIME: 25 MINUTES, **COOK TIME:** 15 MINUTES, **SERVES:** 2

INGREDIENTS:
- 6 ounces (170 g) chicken fillet, chopped
- 2 ounces (57 g) zucchini, spiralized
- 2 cups water
- 1 tbsp. coconut aminos
- ½ tsp. salt

DIRECTIONS:
1. Pour water in the Instant Pot. Add chopped chicken fillet and salt. Close the lid.
2. Select Manual mode and set cooking time for 15 minutes on High Pressure.
3. When cooking is complete, perform a natural pressure release for 10 minutes, then release any remaining pressure. Open the lid.
4. Fold in the zoodles and coconut aminos.
5. Leave the soup for 10 minutes to rest. Serve warm.

Nutrition Info per Serving:
Calories: 148, Protein: 27 g, Fat: 3 g, Carbohydrates: 3 g, Fiber: 1 g, Sugar: 2 g, Sodium: 622 mg

Beef and Cabbage Stew

PREP TIME: 10 MINUTES, **COOK TIME:** 36 MINUTES, **SERVES:** 10

INGREDIENTS:
- 2 tbsps. olive oil
- 3 lbs. chuck roast
- 1 small cabbage head, chopped
- 2 onions, sliced
- 6 cups water
- 1 garlic clove, minced
- Salt and pepper, to taste

DIRECTIONS:
1. Press the Sauté button on the Instant Pot and heat the olive oil.
2. Sauté the onions and garlic for 2 minutes until fragrant.
3. Add the chuck roast and sauté for 3 minutes or until lightly browned.
4. Pour in the water and sprinkle salt and pepper for seasoning.
5. Lock the lid. Set on the Manual mode, then set the timer to 30 minutes at High Pressure.
6. When the timer goes off, do a natural pressure release, then release any remaining pressure.
7. Carefully open the lid. Press the Sauté button and add the cabbage.
8. Allow to simmer for 3 minutes.
9. Serve warm.

Nutrition Info per Serving:
Calories: 337, Protein: 29 g, Fat: 23 g, Carbohydrates: 7 g, Fiber: 2 g, Sugar: 3 g, Sodium: 74 mg

Carrot and Mushroom Soup

PREP TIME: 10 MINUTES, **COOK TIME:** 8 HOURS, **SERVES:** 6

INGREDIENTS:
- 1 pound (454 g) fresh mushrooms, quartered
- 1 onion, finely chopped
- 1 carrot, peeled and finely chopped
- 1 fennel bulb, finely chopped
- 4 cups (960 ml) low-sodium vegetable broth, poultry broth, or store bought
- ¼ cup (60 ml) dry sherry
- 1 tsp. dried thyme
- 1 tsp. garlic powder
- ½ tsp. sea salt
- ⅛ tsp. freshly ground black pepper

DIRECTIONS:
1. In your slow cooker, mix all the ingredients and combine.
2. Cover and set on low. Cook for 8 hours.

Nutrition Info per Serving:
Calories: 61, Protein: 3 g, Fat: 1 g, Carbohydrates: 11 g, Fiber: 2 g, Sugar: 4 g, Sodium: 356 mg

Thai Coconut Shrimp Soup

PREP TIME: 10 MINUTES, **COOK TIME:** 6 MINUTES, **SERVES:** 2

INGREDIENTS:
- 6 oz. shrimps, shelled and deveined
- 1½ cups unsweetened coconut milk
- 1 cup fresh cilantro
- 2 cups water
- Juice of 3 kaffir limes

DIRECTIONS:
1. In the Instant Pot, add all the ingredients excluding cilantro.
2. Lock the lid. Set on the Manual mode and set the timer to 6 minutes at Low Pressure.
3. When the timer goes off, perform a quick release.
4. Carefully open the lid. Garnish with the fresh cilantro and serve immediately.

Nutrition Info per Serving:
Calories: 360, Protein: 18 g, Fat: 30 g, Carbohydrates: 10 g, Fiber: 1 g, Sugar: 3 g, Sodium: 224 mg

Chickpea, Zucchini and Kale Soup

PREP TIME: 10 MINUTES, **COOK TIME:** 9 HOURS, **SERVES:** 6

INGREDIENTS:
- 2 (14-ounce, 397 g) cans diced tomatoes, with their juice
- 2 cups chopped kale leaves
- 1 summer squash, quartered lengthwise and sliced crosswise
- 1 zucchini, quartered lengthwise and sliced crosswise
- 5 cups (1200 ml) low-sodium vegetable broth, poultry broth, or store bought
- 2 cups cooked chickpeas, rinsed
- 1 cup uncooked quinoa
- 1 tsp. garlic powder
- 1 tsp. onion powder
- 1 tsp. dried thyme
- ½ tsp. sea salt

DIRECTIONS:
1. In your slow cooker, mix the tomatoes (with their juice), broth, chickpeas, quinoa, garlic powder, onion powder, thyme, salt, summer squash and zucchini.
2. Cover and cook on low for 8 hours.
3. Stir in the kale. Cover and cook on low for 1 more hour.

Nutrition Info per Serving:
Calories: 227, Protein: 10 g, Fat: 4 g, Carbohydrates: 41 g, Fiber: 8 g, Sugar: 8 g, Sodium: 463 mg

Kale and Chicken Soup

PREP TIME: 15 MINUTES, **COOK TIME:** 24 MINUTES, **SERVES:** 4

INGREDIENTS:
- 1 tbsp. coconut oil
- 1 lb. boneless chicken breasts
- 1 onion, diced
- 2 celery stalks, chopped
- 4 cups chopped kale
- 3 cups water
- Salt and pepper, to taste

DIRECTIONS:
1. Press the Sauté button on the Instant Pot and heat the coconut oil.
2. Sauté the onions and celery for 2 minutes until soft.
3. Add the chicken breasts and sear for 2 minutes on each side or until lightly browned.
4. Pour in the water and sprinkle salt and pepper for seasoning.
5. Lock the lid. Set to Poultry mode and set the timer to 15 minutes at High Pressure.
6. When the timer goes off, do a natural pressure release for 10 minutes, then release any remaining pressure.
7. Carefully open the lid. Press the Sauté button and add the kale.
8. Allow to simmer for 3 minutes.
9. Serve warm.

Nutrition Info per Serving:
Calories: 182, Protein: 28 g, Fat: 6 g, Carbohydrates: 5 g, Fiber: 1 g, Sugar: 2 g, Sodium: 118 mg

Salmon and Spinach Stew

PREP TIME: 5 MINUTES, **COOK TIME:** 13 MINUTES, **SERVES:** 9

INGREDIENTS:
- 2 tbsps. olive oil
- 3 lbs. salmon fillets
- 3 cups spinach leaves
- 3 cups water
- 3 garlic cloves, minced
- Salt and pepper, to taste

DIRECTIONS:
1. Press the Sauté button on the Instant Pot and heat the olive oil.
2. Sauté the garlic for a minute until fragrant.
3. Add the water and salmon fillets. Sprinkle salt and pepper for seasoning.
4. Lock the lid. Set on the Manual mode, then set the timer to 10 minutes at Low Pressure.
5. When the timer goes off, perform a quick release.
6. Carefully open the lid. Press the Sauté button and add the spinach.
7. Allow to simmer for 3 minutes.
8. Serve warm.

Nutrition Info per Serving:
Calories: 264, Protein: 35 g, Fat: 13 g, Carbohydrates: 3 g, Fiber: 1 g, Sugar: 0 g, Sodium: 130 mg

Chapter 10: Soup and Stew / 53

Swiss Chard and Leek Soup

⏱ **PREP TIME:** 12 MINUTES, **COOK TIME:** 6 MINUTES, **SERVES:** 4

🍽 **INGREDIENTS:**
- 8 cups chopped Swiss chard
- 3 leeks, chopped
- 1 cup unsweetened coconut milk
- 1½ cups low-sodium chicken stock
- Salt, to taste

👨‍🍳 **DIRECTIONS:**
1. In the Instant Pot, mix the chard with leeks, salt, stock and coconut milk, stir to combine well.
2. Lock the lid. Select the Manual mode, then set the timer for 6 minutes at High Pressure.
3. Once the timer goes off, do a quick pressure release.
4. Carefully open the lid. Allow to cool for a few minutes, then pour the soup in an immersion blender and process until smooth. Ladle the soup into bowls and serve.

Nutrition Info per Serving:
Calories: 143, Protein: 6 g, Fat: 9 g, Carbohydrates: 13 g, Fiber: 4 g, Sugar: 1 g, Sodium: 295 mg

---

Turkey Meatball and Kale Soup

⏱ **PREP TIME:** 15 MINUTES, **COOK TIME:** 7 TO 8 HOURS, **SERVES:** 6

🍽 **INGREDIENTS:**
- 1 pound (454 g) ground turkey breast
- 1 egg, beaten
- 1 pound (454 g) kale, tough stems removed, leaves chopped
- 1½ cups cooked brown rice
- 1 onion, grated
- 6 cups (1440 ml) low-sodium poultry broth, or store bought
- 1 tsp. garlic powder
- 1 tsp. sea salt, divided
- ¼ cup chopped fresh parsley
- ⅛ tsp. freshly ground black pepper
- Pinch red pepper flakes

👨‍🍳 **DIRECTIONS:**
1. In a small bowl, combine the turkey breast, egg, garlic powder, ½ tsp. of sea salt, rice, onion and parsley.
2. Roll the mixture into ½-inch meatballs and put them in the slow cooker.
3. Add the broth, red pepper flakes, black pepper, and the remaining ½ tsp. of sea salt.
4. Cover and cook on low for 7 to 8 hours.
5. Stir in the kale an hour before serving. Cover and cook until the kale wilts.

Nutrition Info per Serving:
Calories: 228, Protein: 28 g, Fat: 5 g, Carbohydrates: 21 g, Fiber: 4 g, Sugar: 2 g, Sodium: 536 mg

Chapter 10: Soup and Stew

CHAPTER 11: DRINKS AND SMOOTHIES

Summer Cucumber Smoothie

PREP TIME: 3 MINUTES, **COOK TIME:** 0 MINUTES, **SERVES:** 2

INGREDIENTS:
- 1 large English cucumber, washed and cut into chunks
- 1 cup water, plus more if necessary
- ¼ cup mint leaves
- Juice of ½ large lemon
- 1 tsp. fresh ginger, grated
- 1 cup ice cubes

DIRECTIONS:
1. Combine the cucumber, ginger, water, lemon juice, and mint in a blender. Blend until smooth.
2. Add the ice and blend until smooth, adding more water if too thick.
3. Pour to bowls and serve.

Nutrition Info per Serving:
Calories: 25, Protein: 1 g, Fat: 0 g, Carbohydrates: 6 g, Fiber: 1 g, Sugar: 2 g, Sodium: 5 mg

Hemp Seed Milk

PREP TIME: 5 MINUTES, PLUS 20 MINUTES SOAKING TIME, **COOK TIME:** 5 MINUTES, **SERVES:** 4

INGREDIENTS:
- 4 cups water
- 1 cup hemp seeds, hulled
- ½ tsp. vanilla extract
- ¼ tsp. salt
- ¼ tsp. stevia

DIRECTIONS:
1. In a blender, place the hemp seeds and water. Soak for 20 minutes.
2. Blend on high for 1 minute.
3. Add the stevia, vanilla, and salt. Process on high speed for 30 seconds more.
4. If you prefer creamier texture, pour the mixture through a fine-mesh strainer, nut milk bag, or cheesecloth over a bowl.
5. Evenly portion into 4 half-pint Mason jars with lids.

Nutrition Info per Serving:
Calories: 125, Protein: 7 g, Fat: 10 g, Carbohydrates: 2 g, Fiber: 1 g, Sugar: 0 g, Sodium: 95 mg

Avocado Smoothie

🕐 **PREP TIME:** 5 MINUTES, **COOK TIME:** 5 MINUTES, **SERVES:** 2

INGREDIENTS:
- 1½ cups (360 ml) low-fat milk
- 1 large avocado
- 1 tsp. liquid stevia

DIRECTIONS:
1. Put all ingredients in your blender and mix until smooth and creamy. Serve immediately.

Nutrition Info per Serving:
Calories: 245, Protein: 7 g, Fat: 15 g, Carbohydrates: 15 g, Fiber: 7 g, Sugar: 8 g, Sodium: 105 mg

....

Energy Booster

🕐 **PREP TIME:** 5 MINUTES, **COOK TIME:** 1 MINUTE, **SERVES:** 2

INGREDIENTS:
- 1½ cups coconut water
- 1 cup loosely packed baby kale, spinach, or other greens
- 1 cup cherries, frozen
- ½ cup blueberries, frozen
- 2 tbsps. chia seeds
- 2 tbsps. almond butter
- 1 tbsp. lemon juice, freshly squeezed
- 1 tbsp. hemp seeds
- ½–1 cup ice

DIRECTIONS:
1. Place all the ingredients in the blender pitcher in the order listed.
2. Blend for 20 seconds on low, then turn to high for another 40 to 60 seconds or until the mixture is completely smooth. Add more water if you prefer a runnier consistency.

Nutrition Info per Serving:
Calories: 230, Protein: 6 g, Fat: 12 g, Carbohydrates: 27 g, Fiber: 8 g, Sugar: 15 g, Sodium: 90 mg

56 \ Chapter 11: Drinks and Smoothies

Peanut Butter Papaya Chocolate Smoothie

PREP TIME: 5 MINUTES, **COOK TIME:** 0 MINUTES, **SERVES:** 2

INGREDIENTS:
- ¾ cup unsweetened peanut milk
- ¾ cup unsweetened almond milk
- ¼ cup frozen avocado
- ¼ medium papaya, preferably frozen
- 1 tbsp. unsweetened cocoa powder
- 1 tbsp. peanut butter
- 1 tbsp. sesame

DIRECTIONS:
1. Mix all the ingredients in a food processor and puree to combine.

Nutrition Info per Serving:
Calories: 210, Protein: 6 g, Fat: 15 g, Carbohydrates: 16 g, Fiber: 5 g, Sugar: 5 g, Sodium: 105 mg

Vanilla Cold Butter Latte

PREP TIME: 3 MINUTES, **COOK TIME:** 2 MINUTES, **SERVES:** 1

INGREDIENTS:
- 2 tsps. coconut oil
- 1 cup (235 ml) cold coffee, strong-brewed
- ¼ cup (60 ml) unsweetened almond milk
- ½ tsp. grass-fed butter, unsalted
- ¼ tsp. cinnamon, ground
- ⅛ tsp. vanilla extract
- ⅛ tsp. liquid stevia (optional)
- Ice cubes for serving

DIRECTIONS:
1. Add the cold coffee, almond milk, cinnamon, vanilla, coconut oil, butter, and sweetener (optional) to the blender pitcher.
2. Blend until smooth, fully combined, and foaming. Transfer into a cup filled with ice. Serve immediately.

Nutrition Info per Serving:
Calories: 140, Protein: 1 g, Fat: 14 g, Carbohydrates: 2 g, Fiber: 1 g, Sugar: 0 g, Sodium: 120 mg

Chapter 11: Drinks and Smoothies

Strawberry & Kiwi Smoothie

🕐 **PREP TIME:** 5 MINUTES, **COOK TIME:** 0, **SERVES:** 2

INGREDIENTS:
- 1 cup fresh strawberries
- 2 kiwi fruits, peeled and cut into quarters
- 1 cup unsweetened coconut milk
- 1 cup unsweetened coconut yogurt

DIRECTIONS:
1. Add strawberries, kiwi, yogurt and milk to the blender. Blend on high until smooth.
2. Serve with fresh diced strawberries, kiwis, and a straw as desired.

Nutrition Info per Serving:
Calories: 180, Protein: 3 g, Fat: 9 g, Carbohydrates: 20 g, Fiber: 4 g, Sugar: 12 g, Sodium: 50 mg

Ginger Detox Juice

🕐 **PREP TIME:** 4 MINUTES, **COOK TIME:** 0 MINUTES, **SERVES:** 2

INGREDIENTS:
- 2 cored green apples
- 2 celery stalks
- 1 cup packed fresh spinach
- 1 cup packed baby kale
- 1 (½-inch) piece fresh ginger, peeled
- ½ lemon, peeled and seeded
- ½ tsp. lemon zest, grated

DIRECTIONS:
1. To a juicer, slowly add the spinach, kale, apples, celery, lemon, lemon zest, and ginger.
2. Evenly portion into 2 pint-size Mason jars with lids.

Nutrition Info per Serving:
Calories: 85, Protein: 2 g, Fat: 0 g, Carbohydrates: 21 g, Fiber: 4 g, Sugar: 10 g, Sodium: 35 mg

Chapter 11: Drinks and Smoothies

Spicy Tomato Drink

PREP TIME: 10 MINUTES, **COOK TIME:** 20 SECONDS, **SERVES:** 4

INGREDIENTS:
- 1½ pounds (680 g) tomatoes, quartered (about 4 cups)
- 1 lemon, peeled and halved
- 6 dashes of hot sauce
- 2 tbsps. (20 g) yellow onion, chopped
- ½ cup (120 ml) ice cubes

DIRECTIONS:
1. Place all the ingredients into the blender in the order listed.
2. Start on low and slowly bring it up to high. Blend for 20 seconds, or until the desired consistency is reached.

Nutrition Info per Serving:
Calories: 40, Protein: 2 g, Fat: 0 g, Carbohydrates: 9 g, Fiber: 2 g, Sugar: 6 g, Sodium: 170 mg

Quick Peaches and Greens Smoothie

PREP TIME: 5 MINUTES, **COOK TIME:** 1 MINUTE, **SERVES:** 2

INGREDIENTS:
- 1 cup frozen peaches (or fresh, pitted)
- 2 cups fresh spinach (or ⅓ cup frozen)
- ½ cup nonfat or low-fat milk
- ½ cup plain nonfat or low-fat Greek yogurt
- ½ tsp. vanilla extract
- 1 cup ice

DIRECTIONS:
1. In a large bowl, place the spinach, vanilla extract, peaches, milk, yogurt and ice to a blender and process until the mixture smooth purée.
2. Remove from the blender to a bowl and enjoy immediately.

Nutrition Info per Serving:
Calories: 140, Protein: 8 g, Fat: 1 g, Carbohydrates: 22 g, Fiber: 3 g, Sugar: 11 g, Sodium: 90 mg

Chapter 11: Drinks and Smoothies / 59

CHAPTER 12: SNACKS

Roasted Chickpeas with Herbs

PREP TIME: 5 MINUTES, **COOK TIME:** 30 MINUTES, **SERVES:** 8

INGREDIENTS:
- 2 tbsps. olive oil
- Two (15-ounce, 850 g) cans low-salt chickpeas, drained and rinsed
- 1 tsp. cumin
- 1 tsp. dried thyme

DIRECTIONS:
1. Preheat oven to 400°F(205°C). Mix chickpeas, cumin, olive oil and thyme in a medium bowl. Toss to combine well.
2. Spread chickpeas in a single layer on a jelly roll pan. Roast for 30 minutes, stir.
3. Chickpeas are done when crisp outside and creamy inside. Serve immediately.

Nutrition Info per Serving:
Calories: 90, Protein: 4 g, Fat: 4 g, Carbohydrates: 11 g, Fiber: 3 g, Sugar: 1 g, Sodium: 50 mg

....

Crispy Apple Chips

PREP TIME: 10 MINUTES, **COOK TIME:** 2 HOURS, **SERVES:** 4

INGREDIENTS:
- 2 medium apples, sliced
- 1 tsp. ground cinnamon

DIRECTIONS:
1. Preheat the oven to 200ºF (93ºC). Line a baking sheet with parchment paper.
2. Arrange the apple slices on the prepared baking sheet, then sprinkle with cinnamon.
3. Bake in the preheated oven for 2 hours or until crispy. Flip the apple chips halfway through the cooking time.
4. Allow to cool for 10 minutes and serve warm.

Nutrition Info per Serving:
Calories: 100, Protein: 0 g, Fat: 0 g, Carbohydrates: 27 g, Fiber: 4 g, Sugar: 21 g, Sodium: 1 mg

Buffalo Cauliflower Bites

PREP TIME: 5 MINUTES, **COOK TIME:** 10 MINUTES, **SERVES:** 4

INGREDIENTS:
- Nonstick cooking spray
- 1 egg
- ½ head of cauliflower, separated into florets
- ¾ cup panko whole-wheat bread crumbs
- ½ cup low-sodium hot sauce
- ½ cup low-fat ranch dressing
- ½ tsp. salt
- ½ tsp. garlic powder
- Black pepper

DIRECTIONS:
1. Heat oven to 400°F(205°C). Spray a baking sheet with cooking spray.
2. Place the egg in a medium bowl and mix in the salt, pepper and garlic powder. Place the panko bread crumbs into a small bowl.
3. Dip the florets first in the egg then into the panko crumbs. Place in a single layer on prepared pan.
4. Bake for 8-10 minutes, stirring halfway through, until cauliflower is golden brown and crisp on the outside.
5. In a small bowl, stir the dressing and hot sauce together. Use for dipping.
6. Serve hot.

Nutrition Info per Serving:
Calories: 139, Protein: 5 g, Fat: 4 g, Carbohydrates: 22 g, Fiber: 4 g, Sugar: 2 g, Sodium: 392 mg

Asian Chicken Wings

PREP TIME: 5 MINUTES, **COOK TIME:** 30 MINUTES, **SERVES:** 6

INGREDIENTS:
- Nonstick cooking spray
- 24 chicken wings
- 6 tbsps. Chinese 5 spice
- 6 tbsps. low-sodium soy sauce
- Salt & black pepper

DIRECTIONS:
1. Heat oven to 350°F (180°C). Spray a baking sheet with cooking spray.
2. Combine the soy sauce, 5 spice, salt, and pepper in a large bowl. Add the wings and toss to coat.
3. Pour the wings onto the prepared pan. Bake for 15 minutes. Turn chicken over and cook another 15 minutes until chicken is cooked through.
4. Serve with your favorite low carb dipping sauce.

Nutrition Info per Serving:
Calories: 170, Protein: 21 g, Fat: 10 g, Carbohydrates: 1 g, Fiber: 0 g, Sugar: 0 g, Sodium: 498 mg

Peach Bruschetta with Tarragon

PREP TIME: 15 MINUTES, **COOK TIME:** 20 MINUTES, **SERVES:** 4

INGREDIENTS:
- 1 tbsp. extra-virgin olive oil
- 8 oz. (230 g) assorted peaches, halved
- ⅓ cup fresh tarragon, chopped
- ¼ cup low-fat feta cheese
- 4 slices whole-wheat bread, toasted
- 1 tsp. lime juice
- ¼ tsp. kosher salt
- ⅛ tsp. freshly ground black pepper

DIRECTIONS:
1. Mix together the peaches, tarragon, lime juice, olive oil, salt, and black pepper in a medium bowl and toss to combine well.
2. Sprinkle 1 tbsp. of feta cheese onto each slice of toast. Spoon one-quarter of the peach mixture onto each bruschetta.

Nutrition Info per Serving:
Calories: 179, Protein: 5 g, Fat: 7 g, Carbohydrates: 25 g, Fiber: 3 g, Sugar: 5 g, Sodium: 186 mg

....

Spicy Nuts

PREP TIME: 5 MINUTES, **COOK TIME:** 4 HOURS, **SERVES:** 6

INGREDIENTS:
- Nonstick cooking spray
- 2 tsps. liquid stevia
- 1 tbsp. olive oil
- 1 cup unsalted raw pecans (or other raw nuts of your choice)
- 1 tsp. ground cinnamon
- ½ tsp. ground ginger
- ¼ tsp. ground nutmeg
- ½ tsp. sea salt
- ⅛ tsp. cayenne pepper
- Zest of 1 orange

DIRECTIONS:
1. Spray the jar of your slow cooker with nonstick cooking spray.
2. Whisk together the stevia, olive oil, cinnamon, orange zest, ginger, nutmeg, sea salt, and cayenne in a small bowl.
3. Add the nuts to the slow cooker. Pour the spice mixture over the top.
4. Cover and cook on low for 4 hours.
5. Turn off the slow cooker. Uncover and cool down the nuts for 2 hours, stirring occasionally to keep the nuts coated.

Nutrition Info per Serving:
Calories: 204, Protein: 3 g, Fat: 16 g, Carbohydrates: 7 g, Fiber: 3 g, Sugar: 1 g, Sodium: 115 mg

Healthy Almond Crackers

PREP TIME: 5 MINUTES, **COOK TIME:** 10-15 MINUTES, **SERVES:** 8

INGREDIENTS:
- ½ cup olive oil
- 1½ cups almond flour
- ⅛ cup stevia

DIRECTIONS:
1. Heat oven to 350°F (180°C). Line a cookie sheet with parchment paper.
2. In a mixing bowl, combine all ingredients and mix well.
3. Spread dough onto prepared cookie sheet, ¼-inch thick. Use a paring knife to score into 24 crackers.
4. Bake for 10-15 minutes or until golden brown.
5. Separate and store in air-tight container.

Nutrition Info per Serving:
Calories: 171, Protein: 3 g, Fat: 16 g, Carbohydrates: 7 g, Fiber: 3 g, Sugar: 2 g, Sodium: 1 mg

Black Bean Stuffed Mini Peppers

PREP TIME: 15 MINUTES, **COOK TIME:** 20 MINUTES, **SERVES:** 8 (4 PEPPER HALVES)

INGREDIENTS:
- 2 tsps. extra-virgin olive oil
- 1 (16-oz./450 g) bag sweet mini peppers (about 16 mini peppers)
- 1 (15-oz./430 g) can black beans, rinsed and drained
- ½ cup part-skim pecorino cheese
- 1 tsp. dried thyme
- 1 tsp. onion powder
- ¼ tsp. salt
- ¼ tsp. freshly ground black pepper

DIRECTIONS:
1. Cut the stems off the peppers and halve the peppers lengthwise and use a soup spoon and scrape the seeds off. Set aside.
2. Mix the black beans, pecorino, olive oil, thyme, onion powder, black pepper, and salt in a blender and puree 4 or 5 times. The mixture should still have some texture to it.
3. Stuff each pepper half with about 2 tbsps. of the mixture.
4. Serve immediately.

Nutrition Info per Serving:
Calories: 106, Protein: 6 g, Fat: 5 g, Carbohydrates: 11 g, Fiber: 3 g, Sugar: 1 g, Sodium: 190 mg

Chapter 12: Snacks / 63

Roasted Cherry Tomato with Cheese

PREP TIME: 15 MINUTES, **COOK TIME:** 30 MINUTES, **SERVES:** 4

INGREDIENTS:
- 2 tbsps. extra-virgin olive oil
- 2 pints (about 20 oz./570 g) cherry tomatoes
- 8 oz. (230 g) fresh, unsalted mozzarella, cut into bite-size slices
- 5 garlic cloves, smashed
- ¼ cup dill, chopped
- 1 tsp. rosemary
- ½ tsp. kosher salt
- Loaf of crusty whole-wheat bread for serving

DIRECTIONS:
1. Preheat the oven to 350°F(180ºC). Line a baking sheet with foil.
2. Put the tomatoes, rosemary, garlic, olive oil, and salt into a large bowl and toss to combine well. spread on the prepared baking sheet evenly. Roast for 30 minutes, or until the tomatoes are bursting and juicy.
3. Place the mozzarella on a platter or in a bowl. Pour all the tomato mixture, including the juices, over the mozzarella. Garnish with the dill.
4. Serve with crusty bread.

Nutrition Info per Serving:
Calories: 200, Protein: 8 g, Fat: 15 g, Carbohydrates: 14 g, Fiber: 2 g, Sugar: 4 g, Sodium: 250 mg

- -

Garlicky Carrot with Toasted Almonds

PREP TIME: 10 MINUTES, **COOK TIME:** 20 MINUTES, **SERVES:** 4-6

INGREDIENTS:
- 2 tbsps. extra-virgin olive oil
- 1 pound (450 g) carrots, diced
- ¼ cup almonds, toasted
- 1 head garlic (10 to 12 cloves), minced
- 1 tsp. nutmeg
- 1 tsp. sherry
- ½ tsp. kosher salt
- ¼ tsp. red pepper flakes

DIRECTIONS:
1. Preheat the oven to 425°F (220ºC). Line a baking sheet with foil.
2. Mix together the carrots, garlic, olive oil, nutmeg, salt, and red pepper flakes in a large bowl and toss to combine well. Spread evenly on the baking sheet. Roast for 10 minutes, toss, and roast for another 10 minutes, or until golden brown.
3. Mix the cooked carrot with the sherry and top with the almonds.

Nutrition Info per Serving:
Calories: 120, Protein: 3 g, Fat: 8 g, Carbohydrates: 11 g, Fiber: 3 g, Sugar: 3 g, Sodium: 300 mg

64 \ Chapter 12: Snacks

CHAPTER 13: APPETIZERS AND SIDES

Classic Baba Ghanoush

⏱ **PREP TIME:** 10 MINUTES, **COOK TIME:** 20 MINUTES, **SERVES:** 4

🍸 **INGREDIENTS:**
- 1 tbsp. olive oil
- 2 pounds (907 g) Japanese eggplants
- 2 to 4 garlic cloves, peeled and minced
- 2 tbsps. lemon juice
- ¼ cup (60 ml) tahini

👨‍🍳 **DIRECTIONS:**
1. Preheat broiler. Put oven rack at least 6 inches from heat source.
2. Cut eggplants in half lengthwise, and place on a lined baking sheet. Brush eggplants with olive oil. Broil eggplants for 15 to 20 minutes, rotating pan once during cooking. Set aside to cool down.
3. When eggplants are cool, scrape the inner flesh from the skins and transfer to a food processor. Discard skins. Add tahini, garlic and lemon juice to food processor. Pulse about 1 minute until smooth, scraping down the sides of the bowl if needed. Serve or refrigerate.

Nutrition Info per Serving:
Calories: 143, Protein: 4 g, Fat: 9 g, Carbohydrates: 15 g, Fiber: 5 g, Sugar: 2 g, Sodium: 19 mg

Brussels Sprouts with Sesame

⏱ **PREP TIME:** 5 MINUTES, **COOK TIME:** 4 MINUTES, **SERVES:** 4

🍸 **INGREDIENTS:**
- 1 tbsp. extra-virgin olive oil
- 24 Brussels sprouts, halved lengthwise
- 1 cup water
- 2 garlic cloves, finely chopped
- 1 tbsp. roasted sesame seeds
- 1 tbsp. balsamic vinegar
- 1 tsp. kosher salt
- ½ tsp. freshly ground black pepper

👨‍🍳 **DIRECTIONS:**
1. Place the Brussels sprouts in the steamer basket. Pour the water and insert the trivet in the Instant Pot. Place the basket on the trivet.
2. Set the lid in place. Select the Manual mode and set the cooking time for 1 minute on High Pressure. When the timer goes off, do a quick pressure release. Carefully open the lid.
3. Using tongs, carefully transfer the Brussels sprouts to a serving plate. Discard the water and wipe the inner pot dry.
4. Press the Sauté button on the Instant Pot and heat the oil. Add the garlic and sauté for 1 minute. Add the Brussels sprouts, vinegar, salt, and pepper, and sauté for 2 minutes. Sprinkle with the roasted sesame seeds and serve hot.

Nutrition Info per Serving:
Calories: 100, Protein: 4 g, Fat: 5 g, Carbohydrates: 10 g, Fiber: 4 g, Sugar: 2 g, Sodium: 198 mg

Smokey Garbanzo Mash

PREP TIME: 5 MINUTES, **COOK TIME:** 20 MINUTES, **SERVES:** 6

INGREDIENTS:

- 2 cups dried garbanzo beans
- ¼ cup fresh parsley
- ¼ cup unsweetened coconut milk
- 1 tbsp. liquid smoke
- 1 tsp. smoked paprika
- ½ tsp. cayenne powder
- ½ tsp. salt
- 1 tsp. black pepper

DIRECTIONS:

1. Place the garbanzo beans in the Instant Pot and add enough water just to cover. Sprinkle in the liquid smoke and stir.
2. Lock the lid. Select the Bean/Chili mode and set the cooking time for 20 minutes on High Pressure. Once the timer goes off, perform a natural pressure release for 10 minutes, then release any remaining pressure. Carefully open the lid. Drain off any excess liquid.
3. Add the salt, black pepper, smoked paprika, cayenne powder, fresh parsley and coconut milk to the garbanzo beans.
4. Use an immersion blender or a potato masher to mash the garbanzo beans to a desired consistency.
5. Serve immediately.

Nutrition Info per Serving:
Calories: 178, Protein: 8 g, Fat: 5 g, Carbohydrates: 26 g, Fiber: 7 g, Sugar: 1 g, Sodium: 207 mg

---

Cilantro Lime Cauliflower Rice

PREP TIME: 5 MINUTES, **COOK TIME:** 5 MINUTES, **SERVES:** 4

INGREDIENTS:

- 1 tbsp. olive oil
- 1 head cauliflower, chopped
- ¼ cup cilantro, chopped
- Juice of 1 lime
- Salt

DIRECTIONS:

1. Place the cauliflower in a blender. Pulse until small, rice-like pieces form. Alternatively, you can mince the cauliflower.
2. Heat the oil over medium heat in a large skillet. Sauté the cauliflower for 3 to 5 minutes.
3. Remove from the heat. Add the lime juice, cilantro, and salt.

Nutrition Info per Serving:
Calories: 52, Protein: 3 g, Fat: 3 g, Carbohydrates: 6 g, Fiber: 2 g, Sugar: 1 g, Sodium: 24 mg

Chapter 13: Appetizers and Sides

Steamed Artichoke with Aioli Sauce

PREP TIME: 10 MINUTES, **COOK TIME:** 15 MINUTES, **SERVES:** 2

INGREDIENTS:
- 1 cup water
- 1 large artichoke
- ½ lemon
- For the the Aioli Dipping Sauce:
- ½ cup raw cashews, soaked overnight or 2 hours in hot water
- 2 cloves garlic
- 1½ tbsps. Dijon mustard
- 1 tbsp. apple cider vinegar
- Juice of ½ lemon
- Pinch of ground turmeric
- ½ tsp. sea salt
- ⅓ cup water

DIRECTIONS:
1. Fit the inner pot with the trivet and add 1 cup water. Trim the artichoke stem so that it is 1 to 2 inches long, and trim about 1 inch off the top. Squeeze the lemon juice over the top of the artichoke and add the lemon rind to the water. Place the artichoke, top-side down, on the trivet.
2. Set the lid in place. Select the Steam mode and set the cooking time for 15 minutes on High Pressure. When the timer goes off, do a quick pressure release. Carefully open the lid.
3. Check for doneness. Leaves should be easy to remove and the "meat" at the base of each leaf should be tender.
4. Meanwhile, make the aioli dipping sauce. Drain the cashews and place them in a blender. Add the Dijon, vinegar, lemon juice, garlic, turmeric, and sea salt. Add half the water and blend. Continue adding water as you blend until the sauce is smooth and creamy. Transfer the sauce to a small bowl or jar. Refrigerate until ready to use.
5. Use tongs to remove the hot artichoke and place on a serving dish. Serve the artichoke warm with the aioli.

Nutrition Info per Serving:
Calories: 330, Protein: 10 g, Fat: 24 g, Carbohydrates: 27 g, Fiber: 10 g, Sugar: 1 g, Sodium: 372 mg

Curried Cauliflower

PREP TIME: 5 MINUTES, **COOK TIME:** 13 MINUTES, **SERVES:** 4

INGREDIENTS:
- 1 medium head cauliflower, cut into florets
- 2 tbsps. olive oil
- ½ tsp. curry powder
- ⅛ tsp. salt
- ⅛ tsp. black pepper

DIRECTIONS:
1. Press the Sauté button on your Instant Pot. Add the oil and let heat for 1 minute.
2. Add the remaining ingredients and stir well. Lock the lid and sauté for 12 minutes, or until the florets are crisp-tender.
3. Transfer to a plate and serve hot.

Nutrition Info per Serving:
Calories: 95, Protein: 3 g, Fat: 7 g, Carbohydrates: 8 g, Fiber: 3 g, Sugar: 2 g, Sodium: 50 mg

Sun Dried Tomato Hummus

PREP TIME: 10 MINUTES, **COOK TIME:** 2 MINUTES, **SERVES:** 8

INGREDIENTS:
- 5 tbsps. extra virgin olive oil, divided
- 2 (15-ounce, 425g) cans garbanzo beans, rinsed and drained
- 2 tbsps. sun-roasted tomato slices
- ¼ cup tahini paste
- 1 dried red chile/chile de arbol
- 2 large cloves garlic
- Juice of 2 lemons
- ½ tsp. sea salt
- ½ tsp. cracked black pepper
- 1 tsp. dried oregano

DIRECTIONS:
1. Place the beans, tahini, lemon juice, garlic, tomato, chile, salt, and pepper in a food processor. While processing, drizzle the oil until there are no large pieces and the hummus is smooth.
2. Add more water according to desired consistency and continue. 1 tbsp. water at a time, and taste and adjust.
3. Transfer to a serving dish, top with dried oregano and a drizzle of olive oil, and serve.

Nutrition Info per Serving:
Calories: 210, Protein: 6 g, Fat: 15 g, Carbohydrates: 18 g, Fiber: 5 g, Sugar: 1 g, Sodium: 355 mg

---

Pesto Spaghetti Squash

PREP TIME: 5 MINUTES, **COOK TIME:** 12 MINUTES, **SERVES:** 6

INGREDIENTS:
- 1 (3-pound / 1.4-kg) spaghetti squash, pierced with a knife about 10 times
- ¼ cup pesto
- 1½ cups plus 3 tbsps. water, divided

DIRECTIONS:
1. Pour 1½ cups of the water and insert the trivet in the Instant Pot. Put the pan on the trivet. Place the squash on the trivet.
2. Lock the lid. Select the Manual mode and set the cooking time for 12 minutes on High Pressure. Once the timer goes off, perform a natural pressure release for 10 minutes, then release any remaining pressure. Carefully open the lid.
3. Using tongs, carefully transfer the squash to a cutting board to cool for about 10 minutes.
4. Halve the spaghetti squash lengthwise. Using a spoon, scoop out and discard the seeds. Using a fork, scrape the flesh of the squash and shred into long "noodles". Place the noodles in a medium serving bowl.
5. In a small bowl, mix the pesto with the remaining 3 tbsps. of the water. Drizzle over the squash, toss to combine, and serve warm.

Nutrition Info per Serving:
Calories: 90, Protein: 3 g, Fat: 7 g, Carbohydrates: 7 g, Fiber: 2 g, Sugar: 2 g, Sodium: 210 mg

Green Broccolini Sauté

⏲ **PREP TIME:** 8 MINUTES, **COOK TIME:** 10 MINUTES, **SERVES:** 4

🍷 **INGREDIENTS:**
- 3 tsps. olive oil
- 4 cups broccolini, chopped (about 3 bunches)
- 3 cups baby spinach
- ¼ cup fresh parsley, chopped
- Zest and juice of 1 lemon
- 4 roasted garlic cloves, sliced or chopped
- 3 green onions, chopped
- ½ tsp. black pepper, freshly ground
- ¼ tsp. red pepper flakes, crushed

🥄 **DIRECTIONS:**
1. In a large skillet over medium heat, heat the oil and sauté the broccolini, green onions, and roasted garlic until the broccolini is bright green but still crisp, about 5 minutes.
2. Add the black pepper and red pepper flakes and stir to combine.
3. Add the spinach, parsley, and lemon zest and sauté until the spinach is wilted, about 3 minutes.
4. Add the lemon juice to the skillet and stir.
5. Serve immediately.

Nutrition Info per Serving:
Calories: 91, Protein: 4 g, Fat: 7 g, Carbohydrates: 10 g, Fiber: 4 g, Sugar: 1 g, Sodium: 47 mg

Spicy Mole Chicken Bites

⏲ **PREP TIME:** 10 MINUTES, **COOK TIME:** 4-6 HOURS, **SERVES:** 6

🍷 **INGREDIENTS:**
- 6 (5-ounce / 142-g) boneless, skinless chicken breasts
- 4 large tomatoes, seeded and chopped
- 2 onions, chopped
- 1 jalapeño pepper, minced
- ½ cup low-sodium chicken stock
- 6 garlic cloves, minced
- 2 dried red chilies, crushed
- 3 tbsps. unsweetened cocoa powder
- 2 tbsps. chili powder
- 2 tbsps. coconut sugar

🥄 **DIRECTIONS:**
1. Mix the onions, garlic, tomatoes, chili peppers, and jalapeño peppers in a 6-quart slow cooker.
2. In a medium bowl, mix the cocoa powder, chili powder, coconut sugar, and chicken stock.
3. Cut the chicken breasts into bite-sized pieces and place to the slow cooker. Add the chicken stock mixture over all.
4. Cover the slow cooker and cook on low for 4 to 6 hours, or until the chicken registers 165ºF (74ºC) on a food thermometer. Serve warm with toothpicks or little plates and forks.

Nutrition Info per Serving:
Calories: 230, Protein: 29 g, Fat: 5 g, Carbohydrates: 14 g, Fiber: 3 g, Sugar: 3 g, Sodium: 249 mg

Appendix 1: Basic Kitchen Conversions & Equivalents

DRY MEASUREMENTS CONVERSION CHART

3 teaspoons = 1 tablespoon = 1/16 cup
6 teaspoons = 2 tablespoons = 1/8 cup
12 teaspoons = 4 tablespoons = ¼ cup
24 teaspoons = 8 tablespoons = ½ cup
36 teaspoons = 12 tablespoons = ¾ cup
48 teaspoons = 16 tablespoons = 1 cup

METRIC TO US COOKING CONVERSIONS

OVEN TEMPERATURES
120 ºC = 250 ºF
160 ºC = 320 ºF
180 ºC = 350 ºF
205 ºC = 400 ºF
220 ºC = 425 ºF

LIQUID MEASUREMENTS CONVERSION CHART
8 fluid ounces = 1 cup = ½ pint = ¼ quart
16 fluid ounces = 2 cups = 1 pint = ½ quart
32 fluid ounces = 4 cups = 2 pints = 1 quart = ¼ gallon
128 fluid ounces = 16 cups = 8 pints = 4 quarts = 1 gallon

BAKING IN GRAMS
1 cup flour = 140 grams
1 cup sugar = 150 grams
1 cup powdered sugar = 160 grams
1 cup heavy cream = 235 grams

VOLUME
1 milliliter = 1/5 teaspoon
5 ml = 1 teaspoon
15 ml = 1 tablespoon
240 ml = 1 cup or 8 fluid ounces
1 liter = 34 fluid ounces

WEIGHT
1 gram = .035 ounces
100 grams = 3.5 ounces
500 grams = 1.1 pounds
1 kilogram = 35 ounces

US TO METRIC COOKING CONVERSIONS

1/5 tsp = 1 ml
1 tsp = 5 ml
1 tbsp = 15 ml
1 fluid ounces = 30 ml
1 cup = 237 ml
1 pint (2 cups) = 473 ml
1 quart (4 cups) = .95 liter
1 gallon (16 cups) = 3.8 liters
1 oz = 28 grams
1 pound = 454 grams

BUTTER
1 cup butter = 2 sticks = 8 ounces = 230 grams = 16 tablespoons

WHAT DOES 1 CUP EQUAL
1 cup = 8 fluid ounces
1 cup = 16 tablespoons
1 cup = 48 teaspoons
1 cup = ½ pint
1 cup = ¼ quart
1 cup = 1/16 gallon
1 cup = 240 ml

BAKING PAN CONVERSIONS
9-inch round cake pan = 12 cups
10-inch tube pan =16 cups
10-inch bundt pan = 12 cups
9-inch springform pan = 10 cups
9 x 5 inch loaf pan = 8 cups
9-inch square pan = 8 cups

BAKING PAN CONVERSIONS
1 cup all-purpose flour = 4.5 oz
1 cup rolled oats = 3 oz
1 large egg = 1.7 oz
1 cup butter = 8 oz
1 cup milk = 8 oz
1 cup heavy cream = 8.4 oz
1 cup granulated sugar = 7.1 oz
1 cup packed brown sugar = 7.75 oz
1 cup vegetable oil = 7.7 oz
1 cup unsifted powdered sugar = 4.4 oz

Appendix 2: The Dirty Dozen and Clean Fifteen

The Environmental Working Group (EWG) is a widely known organization that has an eminent guide to pesticides and produce. More specifically, the group takes in data from tests conducted by the US Department of Agriculture (USDA) and then categorizes produce into a list titled "Dirty Dozen," which ranks the twelve top produce items that contain the most pesticide residues, or alternatively the "Clean Fifteen," which ranks fifteen produce items that are contaminated with the least amount of pesticide residues.

The EWG has recently released their 2021 Dirty Dozen list, and this year strawberries, spinach and kale – with a few other produces which will be revealed shortly – are listed at the top of the list. This year's ranking is similar to the 2020 Dirty Dozen list, with the few differences being that collards and mustard greens have joined kale at number three on the list. Other changes include peaches and cherries, which having been listed subsequently as seventh and eighth on the 2020 list, have now been flipped; the introduction – which the EWG has said is the first time ever – of bell and hot peppers into the 2021 list; and the departure of potatoes from the twelfth spot.

DIRTY DOZEN LIST

Strawberries	Apples	Pears
Spinach	Grapes	Bell and hot peppers
Kale, collards and mustard greens	Cherries	Celery
Nectarines	Peaches	Tomatoes

CLEAN FIFTEEN LIST

Avocados	Sweet peas (frozen)	Kiwi
Sweet corn	Eggplant	Cauliflower
Pineapple	Asparagus	Mushrooms
Onions	Broccoli	Honeydew melon
Papaya	Cabbage	Cantaloupe

These lists are created to help keep the public informed on their potential exposures to pesticides, which then allows for better and healthier food choices to be made.

This is the advice that ASEQ-EHAQ also recommends. Stay clear of the dirty dozen by opting for their organic versions, and always be mindful of what you are eating and how it was grown. Try to eat organic as much as possible – whether it is on the list, or not.

Appendix 3: Recipes Index

A
Apple
Crispy Apple Chips / 60
Artichoke
Steamed Artichoke with Aioli Sauce / 67
Asparagus
Roasted Asparagus with Almonds / 21
Asparagus Frittata with Goat Cheese / 30
Avocado
Spinach & Tomato Egg Muffins / 14
Avocado and Egg Breakfast Bowl / 33
Avocado Smoothie / 56
Peanut Butter Papaya Chocolate Smoothie / 57

B
Beef
Beef and Cauliflower / 40
Black Bean
Triple Bean Chili / 26
Pearl Barley and Black Beans Stew / 28
Herbed Black Beans / 29
Healthy Southwestern Salad / 47
Black-Eyed Pea
Black-Eyed Peas and Carrot Curry / 27
Blueberry
Healthy Buckwheat Crêpes / 11
Coconut and Blueberry Oatmeal / 14
Broccoli
Broccoli Rabe with Cilantro and Red Pepper / 24
Crust Less Broccoli Quiche / 32
Broccolini
Green Broccolini Sauté / 69
Brussels Sprouts
Brussels Sprouts with Sesame / 65
Butternut Squash
Spicy Butternut Squash Soup / 50

C
Cannellini Bean
Tomato and White Beans with Spinach / 25
Roasted Eggplant and Cannellini Beans / 28
Carrot
Garlicky Carrot with Toasted Almonds / 64
Cauliflower
Sweet and Spicy Cauliflower / 22
Buffalo Cauliflower Bites / 61
Cilantro Lime Cauliflower Rice / 66
Curried Cauliflower / 67

Cherry Tomato
Rice Cauliflower Tabbouleh Salad / 45
Roasted Cherry Tomato with Cheese / 64
Chicken
Fried Eggplant with Chicken / 35
Chicken and Zoodles Soup / 50
Chicken Breast
Cheese and Spinach Stuffed Chicken Breasts / 35
Thyme Chicken Breasts and Brussels Sprouts / 36
Spicy Chicken and Tomatoes / 36
Creamy Chicken with Mushrooms / 38
Quick Summer Chicken Salad / 45
Thai Chicken Salad / 48
Kale and Chicken Soup / 53
Spicy Mole Chicken Bites / 69
Chicken Drumstick
Jamaican Curry Chicken Drumsticks / 37
Chicken Thigh
Chicken and Veggie Kabobs / 37
Chicken Wing
Buffalo Chicken Wings / 39
Asian Chicken Wings / 61
Chickpea
Roasted Chickpeas with Herbs / 60
Chuck Roast
Beef and Cabbage Stew / 51
Cod
Cod with Asparagus / 15
Cod Chowder with Cauliflower / 18
Cucumber
Egg and Cucumber Salad Wrap / 34
Summer Cucumber Smoothie / 55

E-G
Eggplant
Spiced Eggplant / 20
Classic Baba Ghanoush / 65
Flank Steak
Shredded Beef Salad / 47
Flounder
Baked Flounder with Brussels Sprouts / 18
Garbanzo Bean
Smokey Garbanzo Mash / 66
Sun Dried Tomato Hummus / 68
Great Northern Bean
Rosemary White Beans / 25
Green Apple
Ginger Detox Juice / 58
Green Lentil
Green Lentil and Carrot Stew / 29

H-M

Haddock
Haddock Tacos with Cabbage / 17
Halibut
Parchment-Paper Halibut with Lemon / 15
Hemp Seed
Hemp Seed Milk / 55
Kale
Poached Eggs with Sautéed Kale and Mushrooms / 33
Lemony Kale and Tomato Salad / 46
Energy Booster / 56
Kidney Bean
Herbs Kidney Bean Stew / 27
Kiwi
Chia Pudding with Fruits / 10
Lettuce
Grilled Romaine Salad with Walnuts / 49
Mahi Mahi
Mahi Mahi with Green Beans / 16
Mini Pepper
Black Bean Stuffed Mini Peppers / 63
Monkfish
Monkfish in Tomato Sauce / 19
Mushroom
Carrot and Mushroom Soup / 51

P,R

Peach
Quick Peaches and Greens Smoothie / 59
Peach Bruschetta with Tarragon / 62
Pecan
Spicy Nuts / 62
Pork Chop
Sun-dried Tomato Crusted Chops / 44
Pork Tenderloin
Pork Tenderloin with Paprika-Mustard / 42
Pumpkin
Pumpkin Pancakes / 10
Red Kidney Bean
Red Kidney Beans with Green Beans / 26

S

Salmon
Salmon and Spinach Stew / 53
Scallop
Easy Mediterranean Scallops / 17
Shrimp
Spicy Shrimp Kebabs / 16
Shrimp Ceviche with Avocado / 19
Endive and Shrimp with Walnuts / 46
Thai Coconut Shrimp Soup / 52
Spaghetti Squash
Spaghetti Squash Noodles with Tomatoes / 23
Pesto Spaghetti Squash / 68
Spinach
Creamy Spinach with Mushrooms / 22
Spinach with Olives / 24
Veggie-Packed Scrambled Eggs / 31
Spinach and Feta Omelet / 32
Low-Carb Egg Muffins / 34
Fresh Raspberry Spinach Salad / 48
Strawberry
Strawberry & Kiwi Smoothie / 58
Summer Squash
Chickpea, Zucchini and Kale Soup / 52
Swiss Chard
Swiss Chard and Leek Soup / 54

T

Tempeh
Healthy Tempeh Lettuce Wraps / 41
Tofu
Garlicky Tofu and Brussels Sprouts / 40
Tofu and Broccoli Stir-Fry / 41
Curried Tofu / 42
Teriyaki Tofu Burger / 43
Grilled Tofu Skewers / 44
Tomato
Ratatouille Egg Bake / 12
Classic Shakshuka / 30
Spicy Tomato Drink / 59
Top Sirloin Steak
Beef Tips with Portobello Mushrooms / 43
Tuna
Healthy Tuna Salad / 49
Turkey Breast
Crispy Herbed Turkey Breast / 39
Turkey Meatball and Kale Soup / 54

W,Z

Walnut
Walnut and Oat Granola / 13
Whole Chicken
Spiced Roasted Whole Chicken / 38
Wild Mushroom
Cheese Mushroom Frittata / 12
Zucchini
Zoodles with Mediterranean Sauce / 20
Stir Fried Zucchini and Bell Pepper / 21
Zucchini Fritters / 23

HERE ARE YOUR FREE BONUSES:

6-WEEK MEAL PLAN AND SHOPPING LIST
Paperback PDF

STEP 1: POST A QUICK REVIEW

Qualify to receive the 2 free Bonuses by posting a **SUPER QUICK** review on **AMAZON.COM**
(Optional, but I'd really love to get your Feedback)

POST A REVIEW

or Scan the QR code to Review

STEP 2: GET YOUR QUALIFY

Send your review record to me by QR CODE

Made in United States
Orlando, FL
29 November 2024